Red Sox
Triviology

Neil Shalin

TRIUMPH
B O O K S

Shalin, Neil, 1944–
 Red Sox triviology / Neil Shalin.
     p. cm.
 ISBN 978-1-60078-623-5
 1. Boston Red Sox (Baseball team)—History. 2. Boston Red Sox (Baseball team)—Miscellanea. I. Title.
  GV875.B2S53 2011
  796.357'640974461—dc23

                    2011027448

This book is available in quantity at special discounts for your group or organization. For further information, contact:

Triumph Books
542 South Dearborn Street
Suite 750
Chicago, Illinois 60605
(312) 939-3330
Fax (312) 663-3557
www.triumphbooks.com

Printed in U.S.A.
ISBN: 978-1-60078-623-5
Design by Patricia Frey
Photos courtesy of AP Images unless otherwise noted.

Contents

Introduction

One person's triviology (the reader's) is another person's nostalgia (the author's).

Working on a book devoted to baseball history, this writer came face-to-face with his childhood, having the rare opportunity to speak to some former heroes who turned out to be—as heroes often are—as warm, personable, and candid as you hoped they would be. And they were also generous when it came to sharing their memories and observations about the game they love.

I want to start off by thanking everyone who helped with this project, including Dick Bresciani of the Red Sox, who put me in touch with former manager Joe Morgan and a group of players from my early days as a baseball fan, former Red Sox Ted Lepcio, Mel Parnell, Frank Malzone, and Rico Petrocelli.

Thank you to former Yankee Moose Skowron, Lorraine Fisher of MLB Network, and Bill Seiple, and also to Steve Shalin and Mike Shalin for their valuable assistance and support.

Speaking with the major leaguers, I was reminded of something about my history as a fan that I hadn't thought about in a while. I actually rooted for the Red Sox for a time in the 1950s. In fact, I was for any team that played against the Yankees.

Growing up in New York in the '50s you had three options for a favorite team. The Yankees, Dodgers, and Giants were all still in New York (in case you didn't know it, the Yankees are still there—in the Bronx).

My parents had been lifelong Brooklynites before moving to Queens after World War II, so everyone in my family was a Dodgers fan. I chose the Giants as my team (we'll get to the Yankees in a

The bloody sock of Curt Schilling in Game 6 of the 2004 ALCS. *(Getty Images)*

minute). This was the Leo Durocher–led Giants that featured Sal Maglie, Monte Irvin, Bobby Thomson, and Alvin Dark, and soon Willie Mays, who sealed the deal for me.

But what about the American League?

The Yankees were there for the loving. They had that rich history. Joe DiMaggio was approaching his farewell, and they were working on their second of five straight world championships. That was so predictable it was boring.

But there were plenty of interesting stories in the AL in the '50s besides the Yankees and all their titles. The Indians, with one of the greatest pitching staffs ever assembled, the Go-Go Sox in Chicago, and the Red Sox.

In the '50s, the Red Sox were usually what was then called "a first-division team," meaning they finished in the top half of the standings, usually third or fourth.

They had a good catcher in Sammy White, often some power at first base in Walt Dropo, then Dick Gernert or Norm Zauchin, an all-around star, Malzone, at third, a top-flight lefty in Parnell and some other solid but less consistent guys behind him such as Frank Sullivan, Tom Brewer, Ike Delock, Dave Sisler, and Mike Fornieles. And there was that wonderful outfield of Jackie Jensen, Jimmy Piersall, and the great Ted Williams. Parnell, Jensen, Brewer, Lepcio, Sisler, Malzone, and Harry Agganis were particular favorites of mine.

You always watched the game on TV when the Yankees played the Red Sox. Witnessing Ted Williams come to bat was one of the most exciting moments of every game. As a kid, you could cajole another half hour before bed time, just to see the Splendid Splinter face the Yankee pitcher just one more time. And, of course, he usually delivered, despite the infamous Williams Shift the opposition employed.

He was such a dominant force, and his star quality has lost none of its luster over the years. Any examination of Red Sox history threatens to become just another version of "The Ted Williams Story."

Whenever you speak to a former Red Sox player who was his teammate or someone from another team about baseball, the conversation always gets back to Teddy Ballgame. He was revered by his teammates and his opponents. And if you grew up in the 1950s and read the stories about how difficult he could be personally, you are pleasantly surprised at the respect he engendered as both a ballplayer and as a person. Everyone we spoke to talked extensively about what good company he was, how much fun he could be and how interesting it was just to sit and shoot the breeze with him.

In this book, I tried to spread the fame around and present short features and questions and answers on a wide selection of Red Sox, many of whom may not have gotten the credit they deserved for brilliant careers.

I hope you find it as much fun to read as I did to write.

Good luck!

One

First Base

The Rankings!

1. Jimmie Foxx
2. David Ortiz
3. Mo Vaughn
4. Kevin Youkilis
5. George Scott
6. Adrian Gonzalez
7. Bill Buckner
8. Stuffy McGinnis
9. Phil Todt
10. Walt Dropo
HM. Dick Gernert
HM. Kevin Millar

We're in trouble right from the beginning. Foxx had some great years in Boston, but he was better in Philadelphia. However, he's Jimmie Foxx and you've got to respect that. Our No. 2 guy Ortiz hasn't played much first base, but we're not doing a whole chapter

Manny Ramirez congratulates David Ortiz after another monster home run. *(Getty Images)*

about designated hitters, and Big Papi could be the best of all time. But Foxx played the position, so he gets the No. 1 spot.

Vaughn is solid at No. 3, but we give the edge to Ortiz because he's been "the man" in what has turned out to be the Red Sox Golden Age.

Youkilis has been playing first base for the past few years and has done a great job both with the bat and in the field. However, by the time you read this he will have established himself back at third base, where he wasn't as good. Gonzalez was the big pick-up and, based on his past production, he could be near the top of the list by the end of the year.

We're comfortable with Scott at No. 5. He won eight Gold Gloves (three in Boston) and was a force with the bat. After Gonzalez we have a group of six players who all contributed to the cause but none for a full career in Boston.

This was supposed to be a Top Ten, but we couldn't decide who to drop, so we kept everyone. Buckner was certainly better than that one play. McGinnis has gotten some Hall of Fame support from the veterans committee for a career that started with the famous $100,000 infield of the Philadelphia Athletics in the early 1910s, before he spent four seasons with the Sox.

Todt was a fair hitter, but one of the top defensive first basemen of his day. Dropo did have that great rookie season, even though he was gone a few years later. Gernert was a good slugger who had the respect of his Red Sox teammates, who believed that he was handled all wrong by the organization and that he was probably better than his record. And Millar was a major player on "The Idiots" who finally broke "The Curse of the Bambino."

So, we've got a Top 12.

Kevin Youklis

Kevin Youkilis is a throwback to the days of baggy flannel uniforms and scrappy Gas House Gang baseball, a time when there was a giant tobacco chaw stuffed in almost every player's cheek. He's one of the game's hard-nosed players, who doesn't take a brush-back pitch lying down and who plays through pain and disappointment. But he's also the epitome of the modern player, the guy who managers and new-age statisticians are looking to for on-base percentage and clutch hitting.

Youkilis has spent four years as the Red Sox first baseman, where he's distinguished himself by setting a record for most consecutive errorless ball games and won a Gold Glove. But in 2011 he was moved back to his original position at the hot corner to make room in the lineup for Adrian Gonzalez, who was acquired in the off-season from the San Diego Padres.

Youkilis considers himself a third baseman and has, in fact, filled in at third multiple times every year when he was needed.

"Hopefully, Adrian Gonzalez is here a long time, and hopefully I'll play at third the rest of my career," Youkilis said recently. "It would be cool to both start my career and end it there."

And, as we look forward to the 2011 season, there's every reason to believe that Youkilis, who turned 32 in March, will continue his high production and will contribute in all the little ways to help the Sox in their quest for their third title in the past eight seasons.

Youk's rise to stardom as a Boston icon has been a mild surprise to fans who expect their diamond heroes to be graceful like Joe DiMaggio, elegant like Ted Williams, fast and fluid like Ken Griffey Jr., and/or chiseled and muscular like the products of the steroid era.

When he was drafted in the eighth round after a brilliant career at Cincinnati University, there were some doubts due to his thick body (he was heavier then) and lack of outstanding speed.

At times he's been described as roly-poly or pudgy, or as the *Boston Globe*'s Jackie MacMullen wrote, "He does not look like an MVP candidate, more like a refrigerator repairman, a butcher, the man selling hammers behind the counter at the True Value hardware store."

Last season, a year that was shortened by a thumb injury, Youkilis hit .307 with 19 home runs, 62 RBIs, scored 77 runs, and had an OBP of .411, thanks to his ability to draw walks. That ability has earned him the nickname "The Greek God of Walks."

"He's going to work the count about as good as any hitter in baseball," said Red Sox manager Terry Francona.

His patience at the plate is reflected in his perennial place among the league leaders in walks, pitches per plate appearance, and being hit by pitches. And when he does swing, Youkilis usually puts the ball in play, often smashing line drives and hitting into the gaps.

He's been called an "on-base machine."

He has also consistently been among the league leaders in sacrifice flies, as well as batting average with runners on base and in scoring position, and bases advanced on fly balls, passed balls, wild pitches, and balks.

Youk has been equally productive in the postseason, hitting for a .306 average with six homers, 17 RBIs, and an OBP of .376.

He has been to the All-Star Game three times, won the Gold Glove Award in 2007, and was named the Red Sox MVP in 2009.

"Youk fooled all of us," said former Red Sox manager Joe Morgan. "Not one person in the Red Sox chain thought he would be this kind of player and hitter. He's so good it's unbelievable."

The Golden Greek

First baseman Harry Agganis was a legend in Boston before he ever donned a Red Sox uniform.

People who saw him play agree that had tragedy not struck, he would have become an all-star first baseman .

The native of Lynn, Massachusetts, was an All-American quarterback at Boston University. While there he set the school's all-time passing record, 1,402 yards for the season. In those days of ironman football he also had nine interceptions as a defensive back.

After being drafted in the first round by the Cleveland Browns, then the dominant team in the NFL, in the 1952 NFL draft, Agganis turned down a $25,000 bonus offer from the Browns to sign with the hometown Red Sox as a first baseman for $35,000.

He spent a year at Louisville (Triple A) where he hit .281 with 23 home runs and 108 RBIs, and he was called up to the Red Sox in the spring of 1954. He established himself as an agile and outstanding fielder, but had limited success at the plate, hitting .251 with 11 homers and 57 RBIs.

Teammate Ted Lepcio, who'd been close to Agganis from their days at a college prospect camp in 1949, recently talked about the Golden Greek.

"Harry was a true athlete, a great hustler, and a great competitor," said Lepcio. "He was an outgoing guy who was full of life."

Agganis got off to a fast start in his second season and began to look as though he would develop into a competent contact hitter who could spray balls to all fields, and eventually hit with some power.

He was hitting above .300 when he was hospitalized for 10 days in May with pneumonia. Agganis continued to suffer with a cough and fever and was back in the hospital in June, and on June 27, he died of a pulmonary embolism.

"Billy Consolo, George Susce, and I went to visit Harry in the hospital the day before he died," Lepcio said. "We were leaving that night for an exhibition game in Pittsburgh, and we spent some time with him just chatting and joking around. But he kidded that it hurt when he laughed."

The next day in Pittsburgh the Red Sox got the word that Agganis had died.

"We were fairly close as friends and roommates," Lepcio said. "We'd horse around like college kids, but Harry didn't really go out a lot. He was very devoted to his mother, who was a widow, and he would go home a lot and spend time with the family."

More than 10,000 people filed by Harry's coffin, and many attended the funeral for this hometown hero who was admired by so many, especially by those in the Boston area's large Greek community.

"He was a good fielder and a dangerous hitter," Lepcio said. "Who knows how good he could have been?"

But the memory of the Golden Greek will never die.

Each year, the Red Sox Rookie of the Year is presented with the Harry Agganis Award by the Boston Baseball Writers Association. In 2005, Boston University opened its new athletic facility, Agganis Arena, and the Agganis Foundation has awarded more than $1 million in college scholarships to more than 800 student-athletes from Boston and the north shore.

In 1974, Agganis was inducted into the College Football Hall of Fame.

 **Quiz!**

1. Adrian Gonzalez starred for five years with the Padres, but what was his first major league team?
2. Which team drafted Gonzalez with the first pick in the first round of the 2000 amateur draft?
3. Bill Buckner won the National League batting title in 1980 as a member of which team:
   a. San Francisco Giants
   b. Los Angeles Dodgers
   c. Chicago Cubs
   d. San Diego Padres
4. With what team did Kevin Millar make his major league debut?
5. In what year or years, if any, did David Ortiz lead the American League in RBIs?
6. How many times has Ortiz had 100 RBIs or more in one season?
7. What is Stuffy McInnis' real first name?
   a. John
   b. Stuffle
   c. Timothy
   d. Aristophanes
8. Who holds the Red Sox record for home runs in a season with 54?
   a. David Ortiz
   b. Ted Williams
   c. Jim Rice
   d. George Scott
9. Which Met hit the ball that Bill Buckner let go through for an error in the 1986 World Series?
10. How many times in his career did Mo Vaughn hit more than 30 home runs?

Answers

1. Texas Rangers
2. Florida Marlins
3. Chicago Cubs
4. Florida Marlins
5. 2005 with 148 and 2006 with 137
6. Six
7. John
8. David Ortiz in 2006
9. Mookie Wilson
10. Six times (1995–2000). The first four with the Red Sox and the last two with the Angels.

Two

Second Base

The Rankings!
1. Bobby Doerr
2. Dustin Pedroia
3. Pete Runnels
4. Billy Goodman
5. Marty Barrett
6. Jody Reed
7. Jerry Remy
8. Hobe Ferris
9. Mark Bellhorn
10. Bill Regan

Second base has not been the Carmines most decorated position through the years.

We have a legend and Hall of Famer at No. 1 in Doerr. That was a no-brainer. But we're betting on Pedroia as runner-up for his early career Rookie of the Year, MVP, and infield leadership, even though he hasn't played very long.

Runnels and Goodman were both batting champs, but neither was a perennial all-star, though it's agreed that they were under-rated. After that it's a trio of workmanlike players, Barrett, Reed, and Remy, who were loved by fans and did have some impact on Red Sox history. Throughout this process, we tried to err on the side of rating modern guys a little higher because readers might remember them. The roll Bellhorn played in the breaking of the curse certainly earned him his spot.

Ferris and Regan are ancients, the former on great Boston teams and the latter when things weren't going so well.

Dustin Pedroia

Who would ever have believed that Dustin Pedroia would be *this* good?

The five foot nine second baseman with an "average arm and average speed," who was projected as a "dependable major leaguer" by scouts, has become one of the stars of the game and the heart of a Red Sox team that was favored to win the American League pennant going into 2011.

Last season, Pedroia, as well as fellow starters Kevin Youkilis, Jacoby Ellsbury, Mike Cameron, and pitcher Josh Beckett, missed major time due to injuries, and the Red Sox still managed to stay in the playoff race until the final weeks. All are due back to full strength this year, and the addition of prime-time players Adrian Gonzalez and Carl Crawford has the experts referring to the Sox lineup as a juggernaut.

But it is Pedroia, who in his short career has been named Rookie of the Year and AL Most Valuable Player, who personifies the team's aggressive nature and its expectations for a long run at the top. As one observer told the *Sporting News*, "There are few players who embody the traditional image of the gritty, dirtball-type Red Sox player [more] than Pedroia the spunky second baseman."

Pedroia sliding into home for a run against the Yankees. *(Getty Images)*

At the beginning of his rookie year in 2007, while platooning at second base, Pedroia went on a 13-game hitting streak and claimed the job for himself. He went on to lead the team both on offense and defense, won Rookie of the Month honors for May, and ultimately the American League Rookie of the Year Award, hitting .317. In the seventh game of the ALCS, Pedroia's three-run homer and five RBIs led the team to the World Series.

In his first World Series plate appearance, Pedroia socked a home run over the Green Monster, making him the second player in history and the first rookie to lead off the Series with a home run. The Sox went on to sweep the Colorado Rockies with both Pedroia and fellow rookie, outfielder Ellsbury, playing key roles.

What did Pedroia, the Arizona State grad, do for an encore?

In 2008, his second season in the bigs, Pedroia won the AL Most Valuable Player Award. His numbers were impressive. He batted .326 with 17 homers and 83 RBIs, and he tied for the MLB lead in hits with 213. He led the league in runs scored with 118, in doubles with 54, and he stole 20 bases. He also won the Gold Glove and the Silver Slugger Award for second basemen.

In the ALCS he batted .346, including three home runs, but the Sox lost to the Rays, who advanced to the World Series. Last June 24, he went 5-for-5 with three home runs and five RBIs in an extra-inning game against the Rockies.

Pedroia was chosen as an All-Star Game starter in both 2008 and 2009, and named as a reserve in 2010, when he couldn't participate because of injury.

As of the start of the 2011 season, Pedroia is carrying a .305 lifetime batting average with a .376 on-base percentage.

"A lot of people said Dustin couldn't do well," said former Sox skipper Joe Morgan. "They said he couldn't hit. But any guy that aggressive at the plate is going to hit. And on the field, he's made some of the damnedest plays I've seen. The greatest things about him are his determination and his overall love of baseball."

Runnels and Goodman, the Forgotten Batting Champions

Billy Goodman and Pete Runnels had a lot in common.

Both were AL batting champions when they played for the Red Sox and both were capable players at multiple positions. They were slender, left-handed batters with very little power. They both had a great batting eye, could spray the ball to all fields and be patient at the plate, and they both could get on via the base on balls. Goodman stood five foot 11 and weighed 165 pounds, while Runnels was an inch taller and maybe five pounds heavier.

Goodman, whose major league career went from 1947 to 1962, hit only 19 career home runs, while Runnels, who played from 1951 to 1964, was a veritable thumper with 49 career home runs.

Runnels was chosen for three All-Star Games and Goodman for two; and they both finished their baseball playing days in Houston. Both were respected by their teammates for their ability and their character. They were elected into the Red Sox Hall of Fame the same year, 2004.

The two of them were "quiet" ballplayers who have been largely forgotten outside of New England, though Goodman did play in the 1959 World Series with the White Sox—the only postseason appearance made by either of these two professionals.

Let's start chronologically with Goodman, the 1950 American League batting champion with a .354 average, when he was actually a utility man in a powerful Red Sox lineup that included Ted Williams, Vern Stephens, Bobby Doerr, Dom DiMaggio, Johnny Pesky, and AL Rookie of the Year Walt Dropo.

Goodman, who topped the .300 mark five times in his career, played first base, second base, and the outfield, and even had one appearance at third base, the position that became his primary assignment with the White Sox later on. He came in second that year in the Most Valuable Player balloting behind Phil Rizzuto. A lifetime .300 hitter, Goodman also had a career .376 on-base percentage. He later played for the Orioles, the White Sox, and the Houston Colt 45s.

"Billy was a hell of a hitter and a great guy," said Red Sox teammate Mel Parnell. "You could spot him at any position and he would get the job done for you. He swung inside out and found the left-field fence at Fenway to his liking. He was an excitable person, a fingernail chewer during the ball game."

Runnels came up as a shortstop for the Washington Senators in 1951 and flip-flopped between first and second base in the years before he was traded to the Red Sox in 1958. Runnels continued to alternate during his five years in Boston.

In Boston he became an outstanding hitter. He topped the .300 mark six times and had a lifetime on-base percentage of .375. He finished in the top three in batting average in four of his five years with the Sox, winning the batting title in both 1960 and 1962. In his first year he was second in the league in batting.

Runnels' career highlights include getting nine hits in a doubleheader in 1960 against the Tigers (six in the first game, including a game-winning double in the 15th inning), and a pinch-hit home run in the 1962 All-Star Game. He was also a fine defensive player.

"The best thing that ever happened to Pete was the trade to Boston," said former Sox teammate and roommate Frank Malzone. "He was the same kind of hitter as Wade Boggs. He learned to use the left-field wall. He was a professional hitter. He had everything but power. He could run the bases and he was a better first baseman than second baseman. He was also a gentleman, and everyone on the club loved him."

1. When Dustin Pedroia won the AL MVP Award in 2008, he became only the sixth second baseman to win the award. Who are the other five? (Hint: They're all in the Hall of Fame.)

2. Who were the other three second baseman to win the AL Rookie of the Year Award? (Note: Don't count Gil McDougald of the Yankees, who played more games at third base when he won the 1951 award.)

3. In his MVP year (2008), Pedroia finished second in the league in batting with a .326 average. Who won the AL batting crown that year?

4. Who was the runner-up to Pete Runnels when the Red Sox infielder won the 1960 AL batting crown with a .320 average

5. Who was the runner-up to Runnels when he won the 1962 AL batting title with a .326 average?

6. Billy Goodman, who would go on to be the Sox regular second baseman, was a utility man in 1950, the year he won the American League batting crown with a .354 batting average. He played only five games as a second baseman. Who was the Boston starter that season?

7. Who was the second baseman on the Boston Red Sox championship team in 1918, their last title until 2004?

8. Who edged Pete Runnels .328 to .322 for the 1958 AL batting title?

9. In 1950, the year that Billy Goodman won the batting crown, the Red Sox had a team batting average of .302. Only two of their starters failed to hit .300. Who were these two players? (Note: Both drove in well over 100 runs.)

10. Which Red Sox second baseman was named MVP of the 1986 ALCS?

Answers

1. Rod Carew, Twins (1977); Nellie Fox, White Sox (1959); Joe Gordon, Yankees (1942); Charlie Gehringer, Tigers (1937); Eddie Collins, Philadelphia A's (1914)
2. Chuck Knoblauch, Twins (1991); Lou Whitaker, Tigers (1978); Rod Carew, Twins (1967)
3. Joe Mauer (.328)
4. Al Smith, White Sox (.315)
5. Mickey Mantle, Yankees (.321)
6. Bobby Doerr
7. Dave Shean
8. Ted Williams
9. Bobby Doerr (.294, 27 home runs, and 120 RBIs) and Vern Stephens (.295, 30 home runs, and 144 RBIs.)
10. Marty Barrett, who also hit a team-high .433 in the World Series that year.

Three

Shortstop

The Rankings!
1. Joe Cronin
2. Nomar Garciaparra
3. Rick Burleson
4. Rico Petrocelli
5. Vern Stephens
6. Johnny Pesky
7. Everett Scott
8. Luis Aparicio
9. John Valentin
10. Freddy Parent

When you have a Hall of Famer at the top of the list (Cronin) and another one at No. 8 (Aparicio—who is this low because he wasn't in Boston that long) you've got a top ten of pretty fair shortstops.

Cronin started the tradition of hard-hitting Red Sox shortstops that continued with Stephens, Petrocelli, and Nomar, all multiple all-stars. Burleson covered the most ground, and he also appeared in four All-Star Games and won a Gold Glove and a Silver Slugger.

Pesky moved over to third base to make room for Stephens, just as Petrocelli did later when Aparicio arrived.

Valentin became a second baseman when Garciaparra came up, while Scott and Parent were stars on the early Red Sox championship teams.

All in all, this is an impressive group.

Rico Petrocelli

The Brooklyn native who starred at both shortstop and third base with the Sox was what you might call a "throw-forward."

There weren't many home run–hitting shortstops in the 1960s. Only Ernie Banks comes to mind, and he switched to first base for good in 1962. Former Red Sox shortstop Vern Stephens was the cleanup hitter in a potent Boston lineup in the late '40s and early '50s. Years later we would get Cal Ripken Jr., A-Rod, Nomar, Miguel Tejada, and now Troy Tulowitzki and Hanley Ramirez, but in those days Petrocelli was something of a rarity.

Petrocelli—who was also a star basketball player—was a pitcher in high school, a craft he had to give up when he hurt his elbow. He moved into the Red Sox lineup at shortstop in 1965, made the All-Star team in 1967, and was an important cog in the team's "Impossible Dream" year that saw the Sox going to the World Series and losing to the Cardinals in seven games.

"Dick Williams became the manager and he stressed the fundamentals, hit-and-run, bunting," Petrocelli said. "He wanted to change the longtime philosophy of just going for home runs. We were a bunch of young guys—including some people he brought up from Toronto where he had been managing—and we all bought into it."

A capable shortstop and fan favorite, Petrocelli was just as good the following year, leading the league in fielding percentage for shortstops. That set up his big year of 1969, when he hit 40 home runs—a single-season team record for shortstops—knocked in 98 runs, batted .297, and drew 98 walks, which gave him an on-base percentage of .403.

"I was in great shape physically and mentally and had a good spring training that year," Petrocelli said. "I gained 20 pounds of muscle in the off-season. I felt confident. I saw the ball so well, picked it up early and didn't overswing. And I wasn't going to let an 0-for-4 day affect me."

To prove that his monster season was no fluke, Petrocelli hit 29 and 28 homers the next two years with a combined 193 RBIs.

In 1971, the Sox acquired future Hall of Famer Luis Aparicio, and Petrocelli moved to third base, a move he favored because it would be good for the team. Petrocelli came to spring training early that year to work with former Red Sox All-Star Frank Malzone on the transition.

"I worked with Rico down there," said Malzone. "I talked to him about third base. But what work did he really need? He had good hands, an accurate arm, and he knew how to play the game. He had no problems as a third baseman and he did well."

In his first year at the position, Petrocelli led the league with a .976 fielding percentage, a team record that stands today. He also set a major league record for third basemen with 77 straight games without an error. And he had another stellar year at the plate with 28 homers and 89 RBIs.

But that would be his last year as a top power hitter.

In '72 his home run total dropped to 15, but he still drove in 75 runs and continued to play excellent third base. A late-season hot streak by the third-sacker helped propel the Sox into the division race where they eventually finished second to the Tigers.

A series of injuries—including a serious beaning in 1974—hampered Petrocelli over the next few years. He was cut by new manager Don Zimmer before the 1977 season and retired at 33, after a 12-year major league career playing only for the Red Sox.

He currently stands 10th on the Red Sox all-time list in home runs with 210, ninth in RBIs with 773, and 10th in walks with 661.

His nine career grand slams are second only to Ted Williams among Red Sox.

Everett Scott

If only Red Sox owner Harry Frazee had stopped at the trading of Babe Ruth to the Yankees in 1919, there may never have been a Curse of the Bambino, and Boston fans could have continued to support the winning team that thrilled them in the first two decades of the 20th century

But no, in the years that followed, Frazee sent most of his pitching staff and other important regulars to New York as well. Among those traded were catcher Wally Schang, young third baseman "Jumpin" Joe Dugan, and slick-fielding shortstop Everett Scott.

Scott was a light hitter, but probably the AL's best-fielding shortstop at the time. He was the infield leader on the Red Sox world championship teams of 1915, 1916, and 1918. He went on to help the Yankees from 1922 to 1925, and was with the Bronx Bombers for their first World Series victory at the new Yankee Stadium in 1923.

Scott led the AL in fielding percentage eight straight seasons, from 1916 to 1923, and he set the record for most consecutive games played (1,307) that was broken by Lou Gehrig. That streak ran from 1916 to 1925.

His glove work was always a tremendous asset to his team, but it was especially so during the 1916 World Series when Scott led the Sox past the Brooklyn Dodgers.

New York Times baseball writer Hugh Fullerton observed after a particularly fine Scott World Series game: "Where the Red Sox demonstrated their superior ability was at short….At every point of the game where they were about to make a flock of runs, someone hit a ball at Everett Scott. It is bad judgment to hit the ball at Scott... for Scott holds his job by his ability to field, and yesterday he fielded wonderfully."

1. Which Red Sox shortstop jumped to the Mexican League in his early days when he was a member of the St. Louis Browns?

2. Which Red Sox shortstop who won the Gold Glove in 1970?

3. In the 1934 All-Star Game Giants southpaw Carl Hubbell struck out five of the most feared hitters in the American League in succession. Name the Red Sox shortstop who was the fifth and final strikeout in this sequence.

4. Name the Red Sox shortstop who managed the team to the World Series in 1946.

5. Rico Petrocelli was the AL starting shortstop in the 1969 All-Star Game. The first three hitters in the AL lineup that day are Hall of Famers. Who are they, and what teams did they play for at the time?

6. Who was the Red Sox starting shortstop in the 2007 championship year?

7. Vern Stephens led the AL in RBIs three times. How many runs did he drive in for the Sox in 1949, his most productive year?

8. Who was Boston's starting shortstop on opening day of the first American League season in 1901?

9. Who set a major league record for double plays in one season by a shortstop with 147 in 1978?

10. Name the three Red Sox shortstops who have won the Silver Slugger Award as the best offensive shortstop in the AL. The Silver Slugger has been awarded since 1980.

Answers

1. Vern Stephens
2. Rick Burleson
3. Joe Cronin
4. Joe Cronin
5. Rod Carew (Twins, 2B), Reggie Jackson (Athletics OF), and Frank Robinson (Orioles, OF)
6. Julio Lugo
7. 159
8. Freddy Parent
9. Rick Burleson
10. Rick Burleson (1981), John Valentin (1995), and Nomar Garciaparra (1997)

Four

Third Base

The Rankings!
1. Wade Boggs
2. Jimmy Collins
3. Frank Malzone
4. Larry Gardner
5. Mike Lowell
6. Billy Werber
7. Jim Tabor
8. Bill Mueller
9. Butch Hobson
10. Adrian Beltre

Maybe it's not as strong as left field, but the Sox have historically been pretty strong at the hot corner; a tradition that continues with Kevin Youkilis returning to his original position in 2011.

There's a pair of Hall of Famers at the top of the list, and we're giving the nod to Boggs, even though old-timers—really old-timers—will tell you there was nobody like Collins. Malzone and Gardner were both among the best of their eras, while everyone else listed

Wade Boggs doffs his cap after breaking Tris Speaker's Boston Red Sox single-season hit record.

was a major contributors for a significant amount of time. We gave the tenth spot to Beltre as a tribute to how he stepped up and carried the team through an injury-riddled 2010. This position is so deep that we had to omit some pretty fair ballplayers such as Mike Higgins and Carney Lansford.

Frank Malzone

It was clear at the time that the man who won the 1957 American League Rookie of the Year Award was not the person who deserved it.

Tony Kubek of the Yankees won when the baseball writers declared Malzone ineligible for the award because, under the rules of the day, he had made too many plate appearances in his two previous years in the big leagues. Kubek hit .297 with 56 runs scored and 39 RBIs, compared the Malzone's 15 homers, 103 RBIs (third in the league), and 82 runs scored.

"Years later when I ran into Tony," said Malzone, "he would laugh and say 'I stole it from you'. All year long I thought I was a rookie and then the New York writers changed the rules of eligibility in September."

In that rookie year, Malzone also established himself as the slickest-fielding third baseman in the league. In 153 games he had a .954 fielding percentage and also led the league's third basemen in errors, putouts, assists, and double plays. And, as he did many times in his career, Malzone played in every game that season.

After that spectacular rookie year Malzone was awarded Rawlings' first-ever Gold Glove Award for third basemen. For that year only, the Gold Glove was given to one player for each position in the major leagues. The following year it was divided into one winner per league per position.

"I'm really proud of that award because of the company I'm in with people like Willie Mays and Al Kaline," Malzone said. "And because it was the only year you won for both leagues combined."

It may have been some consolation for Malzone that he was named the "Sophomore of the Year" by the baseball writers. However, he didn't find out about this "honor" until 10 years after he retired.

Malzone won the Gold Glove for the American League third basemen the next two years, before Brooks Robinson came along and took the prize 16 years in a row.

As veteran writer Joe Cashman observed about Malzone in a *Baseball Digest* article in 1958, "He's quick as a cat. He covers an amazing amount of ground in all directions. He's in a class by himself on coming in on topped rollers and bunts, picking them up with his bare hand and in the same motion, off balance, and making perfect pegs. The hardest of smashes are soft for him. His arm is the envy of every other infielder in the league."

Cashman called Malzone the best at his position to come along since George Kell (Hall of Famer), and admitted that Kell wasn't as good defensively. In the field, he compared Malzone to some of the greats of all time, such as Hall of Famers Pie Traynor and Freddie Lindstrom.

His steady hitting and great glove work made Malzone—a Bronx native and Yankee fan growing up—a fan favorite in Boston. He went on to play in eight All-Star Games in his 12-year career (11 with the Red Sox).

Malzone was modest when asked about his own career. "I never took a day off," he said.

But former teammate, pitcher Mel Parnell, thought that Malzone was always underrated. "Frank was as good a third baseman as Brooks," Parnell said. "He could make all the plays. But the Red Sox never got to the Worlds Series, and that's where Brooks got all the exposure. Malzone was also a good hitter. He was a fine all-around ballplayer."

After he retired as a player, Malzone joined the Red Sox organization. He's had several assignments, including scouting other major league teams for many years. He's still active as a special assignment instructor. He was inducted into the Red Sox Hall of Fame in 1995 for his contributions both on and off the field.

1957 Major League Gold Glove Winners
1B: Gil Hodges, Dodgers
2B: Nellie Fox, White Sox
SS: Roy McMillan, Reds
3B: Frank Malzone, Red Sox
OF: Minnie Minoso, White Sox
OF: Willie Mays, Giants
OF: Al Kaline, Tigers
C: Sherman Lollar, White Sox
P: Bobby Shantz, Yankees

Adrian Beltre

Things were looking up for the Red Sox at the start of the 2011 season with the arrival of a pair of young all-stars in Adrian Gonzalez and Carl Crawford. The installation of Gonzalez at first made it necessary for Kevin Youkilis to go back to his original position at third after four years of spectacular play across the diamond.

Last year, even though the team was decimated by injuries to key players such as Dustin Pedroia, Jacoby Ellsbury, Youkilis, and Josh Beckett, the third baseman for a year, Adrian Beltre, stepped up and led the Boston offense. After suffering through the worst year of his career in Seattle, Beltre signed for one year with the Sox in the hopes of playing his way into a big contract.

It was only for a year, but what a year he gave them. He led the Red Sox with a .321 average (good for fourth in the AL) and was the team co-leader in RBIs (102) with David Ortiz. He also smacked 28 home runs and scored 84, and finished with a .919 OPS. He led the majors in doubles, with a career-high 49, and he was fifth in both total bases (326) and slugging percentage (.553).

When the MVP voting came around Beltre finished ninth. He was voted the Red Sox MVP by the Boston Baseball Writers Association.

When starting third baseman Lowell was forced to miss significant time because of injury Beltran took over as the team's offensive leader.

"You kind of have to get to know him a little bit, but once that happened he became more vocal in the dugout," said Boston manager Terry Francona. "He became a leader on the field."

Everyone in the clubhouse and the Boston faithful grew to love Beltre. But, as expected, after the season, Beltre turned down another one-year contract offer from the Red Sox and got the big payoff he was looking for with the Texas Rangers, a six-year contract worth $96 million.

"He was pretty honest about what he was doing here," Francona said. "He was coming kind of on a make-good (deal). He made pretty good. It worked out for everybody."

Mike Lowell

Mike Lowell retired after five seasons in which he became one of the most popular players in Red Sox history. He'll be remembered as a solid pro who was a major part of the Red Sox success between 2006 and 2010.

Lowell was acquired from Florida, where he had starred for seven years, including the 2003 championship season. In his first year in Boston he hit 20 home runs with 80 RBIs, and tied for the best fielding percentage in the AL at third base. In 2007 he set career bests in hits, RBIs, batting average, and OPS and was a key man in the Red Sox march to a second World Series win in four years. He was one of four Red Sox players to hit consecutive home runs against the Yankees in April of that year, and his great first half of the season made him an AL All-Star reserve selection.

Then he led the Red Sox to the World Series by hitting .350 during the second half of the season. His 120 RBIs was both a personal best and a record for Red Sox third basemen. His final stats also included a .324 BA and 21 home runs. Lowell finished that

Dave Roberts and the most famous stolen base in Red Sox history. *(Getty Images)*

banner year with a World Series MVP performance, hitting .400 with a homer, four RBIs, and six runs scored in a four-game sweep of the Rockies. He was fifth in the MVP balloting that year.

For the next three years injuries cut into his playing time, but late last season he was honored in an on-field ceremony after playing his last game. Lowell even got a hit in his final big-league at-bat.

He finished his career hitting .270 lifetime, with 223 homers and 952 RBIs.

"When anyone looks back on the successes and memories of the last five years of Boston baseball, they're going to keep running into Lowell," wrote sportswriter Jon Couture.

1. Identify the member of our Top Ten Sox third basemen whose father preceded Bart Starr as the quarterback at Alabama.
2. This Red Sox third baseman is the only man in baseball history to hit two grand slams in one game from opposite sides of the plate.
3. Against which team was this accomplished, and in what year?
4. Who was the first Red Sox third baseman elected to the Hall of Fame?
5. In 1940 this third baseman and three of his Red Sox teammates set an American League record by combining to hit four home runs in one inning. (Bonus: Who were the other three? Hint: All three are in the Hall of Fame.)
6. Who won the American League batting title in 2003 with a .326 average?
7. Which Sox third baseman drove in the winning run in the 10th inning of the seventh game of the 1912 World Series?
8. Name the Sox third baseman known more for his hitting, who won two Gold Gloves as a member of the New York Yankees.
9. Who was the first manager of the American League's Boston Americans in 1901? (He was a player-manager.)
10. Three players on this list also served as manager of the Red Sox. Who are they?

Answers

1. Butch Hobson. His father, Clell Hobson, was Bart Starr's predecessor.
2. Bill Mueller
3. The Texas Rangers, at The Ballpark in Arlington on July 29, 2003
4. Jimmy Collins
5. Jim Tabor (The others were Ted Williams, Jimmie Fox, and Joe Cronin.)
6. Bill Mueller
7. Larry Gardner
8. Wade Boggs
9. Jimmy Collins
10. Jimmy Collins, Johnny Pesky, Butch Hobson

Five

Left Field

The Rankings!
1. Ted Williams
2. Carl Yastrzemski
3. Jim Rice
4. Manny Ramirez
5. Duffy Lewis
6. Mike Greenwell
7. Carl Crawford
8. Troy O'Leary
9. Tommy Harper
10. Mike Menosky

The thing about Ted Williams is, the more you read about him and the more you hear his contemporaries speak of him, the greater he becomes. Arguably the greatest hitter of all time, the Splendid Splinter won the Triple Crown twice, was the last man to hit over .400, and finished his career with 521 home runs; and all of that while giving up six seasons to serve in the military.

That means that Yaz, also one of the great all-around outfielders of the 20th century, must content himself with being in the shadow of Teddy Ballgame, something he probably wouldn't object to.

Those two shadows relegate greats such as Rice and Ramirez to third and fourth. Lewis and Greenwell were underrated stars, and Crawford promises to make his mark in Boston. O'Leary was good for many years, while Harper represented the Sox speed for a brief time, and Menosky, who held the position in the early 1920s, knew how to get on base and could steal when he got there.

Baseball history is loaded with the exploits of Red Sox left fielders. From Ted Williams to Carl Yastrzemski to Jim Rice, members of baseball's Hall of Fame have patrolled the Green Monster for well over 50 years.

Add the years put in by potential Hall of Famer Manny Ramirez and the recent arrival of Carl Crawford—one of the great young stars of the game—and you have a rich tradition of outstanding left fielders.

Mike Greenwell

However, the fine player at our No. 6 position may get a little lost in all the recollections of the high-profile superstars. That's the always-reliable Mike Greenwell. The Gator had some pretty good hitting seasons in his 12-year career while fielding the position and successfully handling the tricky wall. Just like Williams, Yaz, and Rice before him, Greenwell never played for any other team but the Red Sox, and he was always a fan favorite because of his skills, his toughness, and the quiet, unassuming way he went about his business.

Greenwell finished his career with 130 home runs, 726 RBIs, a batting average of .303, and a .366 on-base percentage. He also played in two All-Star Games. The Gator was a tough, aggressive player. He supposedly got his nickname because he wrestled alligators in Florida during the off-season. Former Red Sox manager Joe Morgan said that when Greenwell was 14 there was a bigger 18-year-old boy picking on him, and Mike's dad made him stand up to the older kid and fight him.

"Gator got smoked," Morgan said. "But experiences like that made him tough. We heard the stories about him wrestling bears and alligators."

Greenwell came up from Pawtucket at the end of 1986 and played a little in the World Series loss to the Mets, but he really arrived in '87, taking over left field from Rice, who became a full-time DH. Gator hit .328, socked 19 home runs, drove in 89 runs, and finished fourth in the voting for AL Rookie of the Year.

"He made some mistakes in the field at the beginning," Morgan said. "But he had a good throwing arm and became a pretty good outfielder. Because people remember him as such a good hitter, they assume that he wasn't very good in the outfield. But that's not true."

Greenwell's career year came in 1988, as the team won the Eastern Division before being swept by the Oakland A's in the ALCS. On September 14 of that year he hit for the cycle. He made the All-Star team and finished the year with a .325 BA, 119 RBIs, and a career-high 22 home runs. His OPS was .946, third best in the league.

Greenwell won the Silver Slugger Award in '88 and finished second in the MVP voting to Jose Canseco, who later admitted that he used steroids during his playing days. A few years ago pitcher Curt Schilling was still lobbying for Canseco to be stripped of the 1988 MVP, claiming that Greenwell deserved the award.

He hit .308 and had 95 RBIs the following year, but his homer total went down to 15, and his power numbers would continue to decrease over the next two years. While Gator was always around the .300 mark, he never rose to the level of those above him on the list. He was a line-drive hitter who could reach out over the plate and take advantage of the Green Monster in left. Then, in 1996, when Greenwell was a part-time player, he had one more taste of glory.

In a game against the Mariners on September 2, Greenwell drove in all of the Red Sox runs in a 10-inning 9–8 victory over the Mariners at the Kingdome. It was the MLB record for most RBIs by one player driving in all of his team's runs, and it still stands as a Red Sox record.

Carl Crawford

We've installed Carl Crawford as our No. 7 Red Sox left fielder of all time before he's even played a regular-season game, so we're staking our reputation on the speedy outfielder who was signed after a brilliant nine years with the Rays.

Crawford, who was the MVP of the 2008 All-Star Game, has a .298 lifetime average. He's led the AL in both stolen bases and triples four times, and he's coming off his best power year with 19 home runs and 90 RBIs, which won him the Silver Slugger Award. He also won his first Gold Glove in 2010. He holds most of the Rays career offensive records.

He, along with new addition Adrian Gonzalez, give the Sox an awe-inspiring batting order when added to the likes of Jacoby Ellsbury, Dustin Pedroia, Kevin Youkilis, J.D. Drew, and David Ortiz. With Crawford and Ellsbury—a two-time stolen base champion—the Red Sox can beat you with a versatile offense, capable of smacking the ball over the fence, peppering line drives to all fields, and keeping the opposition alert when they're on the base paths.

"Those outfielders (Crawford, Ellsbury, and Drew) can get the ball" said Sox great Rico Petrocelli. "This is more speed than the Sox have ever had. Everybody likes Crawford. Tampa Bay would have loved to keep him."

And the respect and admiration he's earned extends beyond his skill on the field. Crawford is known as a good teammate, he's active in the community and local charities, he's cooperative with the press, takes his obligation to the fans seriously, is respectful to former players such as Jim Rice, and has a keen awareness of baseball history.

He can often be found around the batting cage and in the clubhouse long after the game, joking around with teammates. He and Ellsbury have a playful verbal feud about who's faster. In short, Carl Crawford is the whole package, and promises to be a Fenway favorite for many years. His former Rays manager in Tampa Bay Joe Maddon pretty much said that at the time Crawford signed with the Sox.

"They're going to love him," Maddon told sportswriter Rob Bradford. "He's going to be embraced. There's going to be a love-fest. He's going to make all types of plays, and do all kinds of stuff where the Boston fans will fall in love with him immediately, so I don't think there will be any type of negative pressure coming his way to perform."

"The man works hard," outfielder Darnell McDonald told the *Boston Globe* during Crawford's first spring training with the Sox. "We've all seen that. He's one of those guys who takes care of business. He's good people."

One person who's not surprised by the attention and praise being heaped on the Sox new hero is Crawford's AAU basketball coach Steve Shalin, who for many years ran the Saluki Basketball League in Houston where Crawford grew up.

The inimitable
Ted Williams

"Carl is a natural athlete," Shalin said. "And he's a really good person. I never knew a kid who made it to pro ball in any sport and seems so well-adjusted.

"Everything you see about him now as a big league player is consistent with how he was when he was a teenager. He was a great team player, and he took responsibility for the team when he was on the floor. He could have gone on to be a quarterback at Nebraska and he could have played basketball in college. He was an all-star when he played for our team, but he couldn't play in the spring because he had to play other sports for his high school because he was so good at everything."

It will be interesting to see if Crawford can move up a couple of slots at a position that has traditionally been the Red Sox showcase spot.

1. Who was the only man in AL history to pinch hit for Ted Williams? (Hint: He also pinch hit for Carl Yastrzemski.)
2. In what career offensive category does Jim Rice exceed Ted Williams?
3. True or False? Carl Yastrzemski is the Red Sox career leader in total bases.
4. In what year did Carl Yastrzemski win the Triple Crown?
5. In what year did Ted Williams hit .406, making him the last major league .400 hitter?
6. How many times (and in what years) did Williams hit 40 home runs or more in a season?
7. How many times did Williams lead the American League in bases on balls?
8. In his seven years with the Red Sox, how many times did Manny Ramirez drive in at least 100 runs?
9. How many times did Ramirez hit .300 or better as a member of the Red Sox?
10. What was the name of the small hill that was in front of the left field wall in the early part of the 20ᵗʰ century?

Answers
1. Carroll Hardy
2. Triples: Rice had 79, Williams 71
3. True. Yaz had 5,539 total bases. Williams was second with 4,884.
4. 1967
5. 1941
6. Once. He hit 43 in 1949.
7. Eight times
8. Six times
9. Five times
10. Duffy's Cliff (after Duffy Lewis)

Six

Center Field

The Rankings!
1. Tris Speaker
2. Dom DiMaggio
3. Fred Lynn
4. Reggie Smith
5. Jim Piersall
6. Johnny Damon
7. Jacoby Ellsbury
8. Doc Cramer
9. Ellis Burks
10. Chick Stahl
HM. Ira Flagstead

The Red Sox have been blessed with a great group of center fielders throughout their history. Speaker, who set the tone, was one of the game's all-time greats, while Stahl, Cramer, and Flagstead were top-flight players prior to World War II. DiMaggio, Lynn, and Smith were Hall of Fame-level producers and defenders who were underrated. Piersall was on their level as an outfielder, Damon was one of the leaders of The Idiots, Burks had some good years in Boston, and Ellsbury's best is yet to come.

As with first base, we're going with more than a Top Ten. We couldn't leave anybody out.

Reggie Smith

If you had to use one word to describe Reggie Smith's career it would be "winner."

The former Red Sox outfielder was the starting center fielder on the Impossible Dream team that went to the World Series in 1967, and he played in the World Series three more times as a member of the Dodgers. In every one of his 13 seasons, Smith's team had a winning record.

Smith was a five-tool player with a sharp mental approach to the game, and that combination made him one of the greats of his era. However, because he never sought glory and publicity, he is one of the lesser-known stars of the past. Except, of course, among the fans of the teams for which he starred.

"Reggie Smith could hit, hit with power, and for average," said former teammate Rico Petrocelli. "He was a good fielder with a great arm. And he was a switch-hitter."

A California native, Smith was originally signed as a shortstop by the Twins, but came to the majors with the Red Sox at the end of 1966, after winning the International League batting title as a member of the Toronto Maple Leafs. When Dick Williams moved up from Toronto as the Red Sox manager in '67, he made it clear that he was going with a young lineup, and Smith was an important part of his plans. Reggie started the season at second base, filling in for the injured Mike Andrews, but he was soon moved to full-time duty in center field.

The Red Sox were in a four-way battle for the pennant that year and finally won the right to go to the World Series on the final day of the season, in what has been called "The Impossible Dream."

The Sox featured a youthful lineup that included—besides Smith and Petrocelli—a 27-year-old Carl Yastrzemski, Joe Foy, George Scott, and Tony Conigliaro. While Smith solidified the center-field spot, he started slowly at the plate and finally began to help the club with his bat later in the season.

On August 20, Smith led the team to a 12–2 win over the Angels by hitting a home run from each side of the plate, a feat he would accomplish six times in his career. He hit the first two of his six career postseason home runs in the World Series against the victorious Cardinals.

In 1968 Smith won the Gold Glove and improved in just about every offensive category. On May 8, Smith made a catch off the bat of Paul Casanova of the Senators that Rico Petrocelli calls one of the greatest catches he's ever seen.

"The ball is going out of the ballpark in center field," said Petrocelli. "Reggie gets there, jumps on the fence, and catches the ball halfway down on the other side, and he managed to not fall on the other side of the fence. Nobody could believe it."

In his eight years with the Red Sox, Reggie batted .286 and hit 144 home runs, with a high of 30 in 1971. He had an on-base percentage of .354 and drove in 536 runs, and he was chosen for three All-Star teams. He led the league in total bases in 1971.

"Reggie Smith was as good a player as we've ever had," said longtime Red Sox Johnny Pesky.

Often the object of racial epithets, the recipient of hate mail, and the target of unruly fans throwing missiles while he was in the outfield, Smith said the Red Sox front office, and many fans, "don't want a black star." He was dealt to the Cardinals for pitcher Rick Wise and outfielder Bernie Carbo in 1974 and would enjoy even better years in the National League, playing nine more seasons there.

He played on three Dodgers pennant winners in his six seasons in L.A. and anchored the Cardinals outfield for three years. Smith finally got a World Series victory as a supporting player for the 1981 Dodgers. He also represented the NL in four more All-Star Games. Smith finished his career with the San Francisco Giants in 1982. In retirement, he worked in the Dodgers organization for many years.

His final stats: .287 lifetime average with 314 homers and 1,092 RBIs. He was the first man to hit more than 100 home runs in each league. Remembering Smith's career, former outfielder Tom Grieve once said, "The thing I liked about him is he could do everything and he looked good doing it. Some guys have maximum effort, they grunt when they throw it, and their head's flying when they're running, but with him everything was smooth.

"When he threw the ball like that it didn't even look like he was trying to throw it. He had an effortless swing, a switch-hitter. He looked good. He made the game look easy."

Jacoby Ellsbury

In 2008 and 2009, Jacoby Ellsbury burst onto the national scene. Between his unbelievable speed, his outstanding play in the field, and acumen at the plate, Ellsbury has established himself as one of the best center fielders in baseball.

The 2010 season was pretty much wiped out for the Oregon native due to injured ribs. As of the start of the 2011 season, however, Ellsbury was healthy and ready to lead off for the BoSox, resuming a career that should move him up our list of Sox center fielders in the near future.

Tris Speaker

Tris Speaker is the standard by which all center fielders are measured. One of the great fielders, Speaker was famous for playing shallow in center—almost behind second base—and having such great instincts that at the crack of the bat he was on his way, and it didn't matter where it was hit.

(Left to right) Boston Red Sox outfielders Harry Hooper, Tris Speaker, and Duffy Lewis

"Tris was the king of the outfield. It was always, 'Take it,' or 'I got it.' In all [those] years we never bumped each other," said outfielder and Red Sox teammate Duffy Lewis.

Speaker, who played his entire career in the shadow of Ty Cobb, was also one of the great hitters of the early 20th century. He finished with a lifetime average of .345, a .428 OBP, 3,514 hits, 117 home runs, and 1,529 RBIs. He won the 1916 batting title while with the Indians, and led the 1912 Red Sox, 1915 Red Sox, and 1920 Indians to World Series victories. He was the seventh player elected to the National Baseball Hall of Fame.

Speaker is the only man in baseball history to have three hitting streaks of 20 or more games in one season, coming through with streaks of 20, 30, and 20 games for the Red Sox in 1912.

Dom DiMaggio

Joltin' Joe's younger brother Dominic—or the Little Professor, as he was called because he wore spectacles—was the consummate leadoff man. He was a .298 lifetime hitter with a career .383 OBP, who played 11 seasons for the Red Sox. A seven-time All-Star, Dom averaged 105 runs scored per season and put together hitting streaks of 34 and 27 games.

DiMaggio's fans believe that the three seasons he lost to military service in his prime have kept him from getting to the Hall of Fame. "I can't understand why he's not in the Hall of Fame," said his old friend and teammate Johnny Pesky, who called DiMaggio "the perfect player."

When he was a member of the Hall of Fame Veterans Committee, Ted Williams lobbied long and hard for DiMaggio to be elected. "He was as good a center fielder as I ever saw," said Williams. "Dom saved more runs as a center fielder than anybody else. He should be in the Hall of Fame."

Fred Lynn

Fred Lynn burst onto the American League scene in 1975 when he became the first player to win both the Rookie of the Year and the Most Valuable Player Award. Lynn led the league in doubles (47, an AL rookie record) and runs (103), and he was the first rookie to ever

Fred Lynn goes deep in the hole to retrieve this fly ball.

lead the AL in slugging (.566). He batted .331 (second to Rod Carew) and was third in RBIs with 105, and fourth in total bases with 299. Lynn also hit 21 homers.

On June 18, 1975, Lynn hit three home runs, a triple, and a single while driving in 10 runs against the Detroit Tigers. Oh, and he hit .364 in the playoffs that year. He would go on to play in the All-Star Game nine times, winning the MVP with a grand slam in 1983. He was named MVP of the 1982 AL Championship Series with the Angels. In all, he hit .407 in the postseason for his career.

"He was pretty to watch," said Lou Piniella. "Everything flowed easily. He had a very pretty batting swing, classic batting style. He had power to left-center and power to right. He played the outfield really well, a complete ballplayer."

Jimmy Piersall

A defensive outfielder comparable to any of those already mentioned, Piersall became a pretty solid hitter as well, but was more famous for his battles with mental illness and his on-field antics than for the solid ballplayer he was.

He patrolled center field for the Sox for six years, taking over in 1953 following Dom DiMaggio's retirement. Most observers felt there was no defensive drop-off with Piersall, who played a shallow center field, a la Speaker.

Piersall played in two All-Star Games. He also led the league in doubles in 1956, while scoring 91 runs, driving in 87, and batting .293. He won the first of his two Gold Gloves in Boston in 1958.

"Jimmy was underappreciated," said Piersall's former roommate Ted Lepcio. "He was a terrific fielder. He didn't have to take a back seat to [Dom] as an outfielder."

"I thought Joe DiMaggio was the greatest defensive outfielder I ever saw," said Stengel, who managed Joe from 1949 to 1951, "but I have to rate Piersall better."

Piersall also famously went behind the monuments in Yankee Stadium and sat down during a game. Also, when he was a member of the Mets, he ran around the bases facing backward after hitting his 100th career home run.

"Probably the best thing that happened to me was going nuts," said Piersall, who was hospitalized in 1952 after suffering a nervous breakdown. "Who ever heard of Jim Piersall 'til that happened?"

He was elected to the Red Sox Hall of Fame in 2010.

**Quiz!**

1. What team did Ellis Burks play for in 1993 after leaving the Red Sox?
2. Name the National League pitcher who served up Fred Lynn's grand slam in the 1983 All-Star Game.
3. With which team did Johnny Damon begin his major league career?
   a. Oakland Athletics
   b. Kansas City Royals
   c. New York Yankees
   d. Texas Rangers
4. Johnny Damon made the AL All-Star team twice as a member of which team?
5. Name the outfielder who batted over .300 for the Red Sox every year between 1937 and 1940.
6. This center fielder led the AL in at-bats seven times.
7. Who set AL records for outfielders with 503 putouts and 526 total chances, both of which stood for almost 30 years?
8. Which center fielder committed suicide when he was the manager of the Red Sox in 1907?
9. Who was the Red Sox center fielder before Jacoby Ellsbury?
10. Who began the 2011 season as Ellsbury's outfield mates with the Red Sox?

Answers
1. The White Sox
2. Atlee Hammaker of the Giants
3. B, Royals
4. The Red Sox
5. Doc Cramer
6. Doc Cramer
7. Dom DiMaggio
8. Chick Stahl
9. Coco Crisp
10. Carl Crawford in left field and J.D. Drew in right.

Seven

Right Field

The Rankings!
1. Harry Hooper
2. Dwight Evans
3. Jackie Jensen
4. Tony Conigliaro
5. Trot Nixon
6. J.D. Drew
7. Buck Freeman
8. Tom Brunansky
9. Earl Webb
10. Al "Zeke" Zarilla

While the Red Sox right field may not be as strong historically as the other two outfield positions—only Hall of Famer Hooper and should-be Hall of Famer Evans played at superstar level for many years—this position would have been stronger if Jensen and Conigliaro had been able to play out there careers to a ripe old age.

Both of these Sox stars could have gone on achieving great things, in Conigliaro's case, for many more years. The Boston Baseball Writers Association present awards each year in both their names.

Tont Conigliaro

Rico Petrocelli was in the on-deck circle as the Red Sox played the Angels at Fenway Park on August 17, 1967, when his friend and teammate, Tony Conigliaro, was beaned in the face by a pitch thrown by Jack Hamilton.

"I saw the ball coming in head high and he didn't move," Petrocelli said. "And finally he moved his head a little and the ball hit him just below the eye. It made a squashing sound like a grapefruit."

Petrocelli rushed to his stricken teammate and comforted him until the trainer and the doctor arrived.

"His face and his eyes were swollen," Petrocelli said. "At first I thought it hit him in the temple and it could be fatal."

The pitch fractured Conigliaro's cheekbone and eye socket, dislocated his jaw, and severely damaged his retina. He nearly died and he missed the rest of the "Impossible Dream" year and the entire following season.

"Tony was so tough at the plate," Petrocelli said. "He'd stand right on the plate and he wouldn't give an inch. We'd tell him to watch it but he thought he could get out of the way."

Tony C. came back to play in 1969 and was named Comeback Player of the Year, enjoying his finest season, with career highs in home runs (36) and RBIs (116). In his first game back, Conigliaro hit a two-run homer in the 10th inning and scored the winning run in the 12th as the Red Sox won their season opener over the Orioles in Baltimore.

But by 1971 his deteriorating eyesight brought his career to a premature end, except for a brief return with the Red Sox four years later.

As a rookie, Conigliaro—a local Boston guy—batted .290 with 24 home runs, and the following year he led the league in home runs with 32, becoming the youngest home run champion in American League history. At 22 years and 197 days old, he became the second youngest player in history to reach 100 home runs. (Mel Ott did it at 22 years and 132 days.)

"Before that accident, Tony had it all on and off the field," Petrocelli said. "He was young, handsome, and talented. The Boston fans loved him. And he was born to play baseball. He could hit to all fields and he had a natural home run swing. With the DH just a few years away he could have played 'til he was 40. I thought he could hit 500 home runs."

When his playing career ended, Tony C. went into broadcasting. But in 1982 he suffered a heart attack and a stroke, which resulted in a vegetative state that would last for the next eight years. He died in 1990 at the age of 45.

Jackie Jensen

Here's a quick trivia question.

Name the Boston Red Sox outfielder who was the first person to play in the Rose Bowl, the World Series, and the MLB All-Star Game.

If your answer is Jackie Jensen, you're correct.

Jensen, an All-American running back at California, where he came in fourth in the voting for the Heisman trophy, originally signed with the New York Yankees as an outfielder, but he became expendable when Mickey Mantle arrived. He then spent two years as a Washington Senator before coming to the Red Sox in 1954. For six years he played right field, most of the time with Ted Williams and Jimmy Piersall to form an outstanding outfield.

But his is another Red Sox story of a career cut short, albeit when he was older and for an unusual reason.

Jensen had a paralyzing fear of flying, and as baseball became more dependent on air travel, Jackie's life became more complicated. "If we had a day game on Thursday in Boston and then had to fly to Chicago to start a series on Friday night, Jackie would go there by train," said Frank Malzone. "He'd say, 'I'll see you guys in Chicago,' and he'd take the train. He was always there in the next city so there really wasn't a problem."

But in 1960, citing his fear of flying and the long separations from his family, Jensen retired at the age of 33. (Jensen, by the way, was married to his high school sweetheart, Zoe Ann Olsen, who was medaled in diving at the 1948 and 1952 Summer Olympics. The couple had three children. They divorced in 1968.)

He returned in '61, but by that time the American League had expanded to the West Coast, which made it almost impossible for Jensen. He tried, though. He hired a hypnotist to help him fight his panic attacks at airports, but it didn't really work. After an ineffective 1961 season Jensen retired again, this time for good.

He led the league in RBIs three times—knocking in more than 100 runs five times—went to two All-Star Games (he had also made the All-Star team once as a Senator), led the league once in triples, and once in stolen bases. In 1958, Jensen was named the AL Most Valuable Player when he slugged 35 home runs, drove in 122, and had a .285 average. That year he had an OBP of .396 and a .535 slugging percentage. He also won a Gold Glove and led the AL in assists and double plays twice each.

Jensen was a great athlete with a right-handed swing perfectly tailored for Fenway Park.

In *My Turn at Bat: The Story of My Life,* Ted Williams writes, "Right field in Boston is a bitch—the sun field—and few play it well. Jackie Jensen was the best I saw at it."

"Jackie had good speed and great power and he was underrated as a base runner," said Frank Malzone. "As an outfielder he made all the plays and he made it look easy. When he threw to me at third from right field he got it there the right way. He was also a great teammate."

After he retired, Jensen went into broadcasting, and for a time he managed in the minor leagues and coached baseball in college. Jensen died of a heart attack in 1982 at the age of 55.

He was inducted into the College Football Hall of Fame in 1984 and the Red Sox Hall of Fame in 2000.

1. Who is the only man to play on four Red Sox World Series championship teams?
2. Name the outfielder who was sent to the Washington Senators as part of the trade for Jackie Jensen.
3. Which of our Top Ten right fielders was an original Red Sox "Dirt Dog"?
4. Who was the first player to lead both the National League and the American League in home runs during his career?
5. In 1931 Earl Webb established a single-season batting record that still stands today. What is that record?
6. Who was the only player in MLB history to twice be among four baseball teammates who hit four consecutive home runs in a game?
7. How many Gold Gloves did Dwight Evans win?
8. Who was the right fielder in the Red Sox all-.300-hitting outfield of 1950 with Ted Williams and Dom DiMaggio?
9. With what American League team did Tom Brunansky begin his major league career?
10. Who was the only player in baseball history besides Rickey Henderson to hit a home run to lead off both games of a doubleheader?

Answers

1. Harry Hooper, 1912, 1915, 1916, and 1918
2. Tom Umphlet
3. Trot Nixon
4. Buck Freeman
5. He hit 67 doubles in the 1931 season.
6. J.D. Drew, with the Red Sox in 2008 and the Dodgers in 2007 (see "Worth Noting" sidebar, page 62).
7. Eight
8. Al (Zeke) Zarilla
9. The California Angels in 1981
10. Harry Hooper.

Fisk wills his famous 12th-inning home run to stay fair.

Worth Noting

Major league teams have hit four consecutive home runs only seven times, and J.D. Drew hit the second homer in two of those sequences.

- June 8, 1961–Milwaukee Braves–7th Inning: Eddie Mathews, Hank Aaron, Joe Adcock, and Frank Thomas
- July 31, 1963–Indians–6th Inning: Woodie Held, Pedro Ramos, Tito Francona (Terry's father), and Larry Brown
- May 2, 1964–Twins–11th Inning: Tony Oliva, Bob Allison, Jimmie Hall, and Harmon Killebrew
- September 18, 2006–Dodgers–9th Inning: Jeff Kent, J.D. Drew, Russell Martin, and Marlon Anderson
- April 22, 2007–Red Sox–3rd Inning: Manny Ramirez, J.D. Drew, Mike Lowell, and Jason Varitek
- August 14, 2008–White Sox–1st Inning: Jim Thome, Paul Konerko, Alexei Ramirez, and Juan Uribe
- August 11, 2010–Diamondbacks–4th Inning: Adam LaRoche, Miguel Montero, Mark Reynolds, and Stephen Drew (J.D.'s brother)

Eight

Catcher

The Rankings!
1. Carlton Fisk
2. Jason Varitek
3. Sammy White
4. Rick Ferrell
5. Rich Gedman
6. Tony Pena
7. Bill Carrigan
8. Lou Criger
9. Birdie Tebbetts
10. Scott Hatteberg

While Carlton Fisk is the obvious standout here, the guys behind him all had impressive careers.

Varitek presided over what has been the greatest Red Sox era since the early 20th century. White was one of the best defensive catchers in the league in the 1950s. Ferrell is a Hall of Famer, who made the All-Star team four times with the Red Sox, and Gedman was a leader on some good teams in the 1980s. Pena was an all-star for the Pirates who wore the "Tools of Ignorance" for Boston later in his career. Tebbetts was the catcher on the great-hitting Sox teams from 1947 to 1950. Carrigan and Criger were great defensive catchers in the early 20th century, while Hatteberg was a slugger who went on to Oakland where he played first base.

Jason Varitek

"Always I am saying good-bye to you, and always I am meeting you again."

> —Alan Arkin to Carl Reiner
> in *The Russians Are Coming, the Russians Are Coming*

All the time Red Sox fans are saying good-bye to Jason Varitek, and all the time they're seeing him again. In fact, in 2010 the fans at Fenway gave him a standing ovation after his last at-bat of the season, figuring that it was the Captain's last day as an active major leaguer. He started the 2011 season as a 39-year-old catcher—having toiled behind the plate for 13 seasons with the Red Sox—who saw 2010 virtually wiped out by injuries.

But spring training started, and there was Varitek, back for at least one more go-round. He went into 2011 as a part-time catcher and full-time mentor to young Jarrod Saltalamacchia, who's expected to provide some offense, but needs the wisdom of the veteran to help him as a defender and handler of pitchers.

"I don't know how he does it, but he continues to do it every year," said Sox manager Terry Francona to ESPN's Joe McDonald. "He works so hard. He's in great shape. I think he's going to excel in that backup role."

"If my body holds up and I'm able to do the things that I feel that I can still do, then I'll play as long as I can," Varitek said. "If I'm not putting myself in a competitive spot to help a team win, then I've got to question things again."

Varitek, a student of the game who is expected to be a manager some day, represents one of the great trade acquisitions in Red Sox history. He and Derek Lowe were obtained from the Mariners in 1997 for pitcher Heathcliff Slocumb, and Varitek started paying dividends the following year.

By 1999 he was entrenched as the full-time catcher, and he's caught 1,420 games in his career, most by a Red Sox backstop. He's also Boston's leader among catchers in home runs (182) and RBIs (721).

Varitek, a switch-hitter, has been selected for the All-Star team three times, and has won both the Gold Glove Award (2005) and the Silver Slugger Award (2005). In 2004 he was named as only the third captain of the Red Sox since 1923, following Hall of Fame members Carl Yastrzemski and Jim Rice in that role. And most importantly for Red Sox fans, Varitek was the starting catcher on two world championship clubs. The first, in 2004, came after the catcher's best season, in which he hit a career-high .296 with 18 home runs and 73 RBIs.

In 2006 he represented the United States in the World Baseball Classic, hitting a grand slam against Team Canada. In September of that year, there was a pregame ceremony honoring Varitek as the first Red Sox catcher to catch 1,000 games. Hall of Famer Carlton Fisk, who had held the team record of 990 career games, presented Varitek with a special award. In 2007, Varitek was the catcher in the Red Sox second World Series win in four years. He has also caught a Major League record four no-hitters. In order they were by Hideo Nomo in 2001, Lowe in 2002, Clay Buchholz in 2007, and Jon Lester in 2008.

Looking back on Varitek's career, veteran Boston scribe Mike Shalin calls him a borderline Hall of Famer.

"He's a leader, no question," Shalin said. "He went through hell with aches and pains. After the game you'd see him all ice-bagged up. Pitchers love him. He's a good defensive catcher and he can handle a pitching staff. But what stands out to me about Varitek is that he's a better hitter than people gave him credit for. He'll get the big hit. There's not much difference between him and (Jorge) Posada and they're talking about Posada for the Hall of Fame."

And he added: "Every winter Varitek is gone, that's it, and he's still there." This year he's helping Saltalamacchia in his effort to become the Red Sox next-generation catcher.

"He's going to be a good player," Varitek said. "He's too gifted and works too hard not to be."

Rick Ferrell

Carlton Fisk isn't the only Hall of Famer among the Red Sox Top Ten catchers. Our No. 4, Rick Ferrell, was selected for the Hall of Fame by the Veterans Committee in 1984.

Though he was a fine catcher and hitter, Ferrell is one of those players from the '20s and '30s whose Cooperstown selection was controversial, as some observers attributed it to cronyism among Veterans Committee members.

Definitely one of the best-hitting catchers in baseball, Ferrell spent 18 years in the big leagues, including more than four years with the Red Sox. He batted .302 for the Sox and had an OBP of .394. He was a patient hitter, working out almost 1,000 walks, and he rarely struck out. He held the record for career games as a catcher with 1,806 until Carlton Fisk broke it in 1988.

Ferrell had a strong throwing arm and led the AL four times in baserunners caught stealing and twice in assists and putouts. And, toward the end of his career, he caught for a Washington pitching staff that had four knuckleballers. He had a fine career, and continued as a coach and executive for many years after his retirement.

In his 18 years in the majors he had a .281 career batting average, along with 28 home runs, 734 RBIs, and an on-base percentage of .378. He hit over .300 four times during his career, and struck out just 277 times in more than 6,000 at-bats. He finished his career with a .984 fielding percentage and he was an eight-time All-Star.

However, there are many who feel that Rick wasn't even the most worthy Hall of Fame candidate in his own family.

That honor goes to his younger brother, Wes. Wes was a volatile character but a talented pitcher—maybe the greatest-hitting pitcher of all time—and he has continued to be considered for the Hall of Fame by the Veterans Committee as recently as 2008. Wes is still the only pitcher in MLB since 1900 to win 20 games in his first four years, which he did with the Cleveland Indians from 1929 to 1932. After a down year, he was united with his brother in 1934 on the Red Sox for an all-Ferrell battery.

In Boston, Ferrell proceeded to win 20 games two more times, posting a record of 62–40 before both Ferrells were traded to Washington in 1937. Wes was an All-Star twice, was runner-up for the MVP with the Sox in 1935, and pitched a no-hitter in 1931. And, as we mentioned before, Wes was also probably one of the best-hitting pitchers of all time, with a lifetime batting average of .280. He also holds the records for most home runs by a pitcher in a season (9) and in a career (38). In 1935, Ferrell won a league-high 25 games and hit .347—only two points lower than the AL batting champion Buddy Myer. He was runner-up to Hank Greenberg of the world champion Tigers in the MVP voting.

Great Hall of Fame credentials, but Wes Ferrell's career was marred by his ferocious temper, as he frequently quarreled with umpires and club executives. He was as unpleasant and volatile as his brother was likeable and even-tempered. Wes would pick a fight with anybody, often without provocation. In 1936, Boston manager Joe Cronin fined Ferrell $1,000 and suspended him indefinitely for walking off the mound during a Yankee rally.

"I don't care if I never see Ferrell again," said Cronin.

Ferrell was furious when told of the manager's remark and said, "I'm going to punch Cronin in the jaw as soon as I can find him."

Throughout his career the press paid more attention to Ferrell's tantrums than to his excellent pitching record. Ferrell hated losing more than most players. When he lost a game he was likely to go into the clubhouse and tear his mitt to shreds. One teammate estimated that Ferrell went through about 10 mitts a year. Billy Werber once said, "I saw him get so mad after losing a game of poker that he tore the deck of cards in half with his bare hands."

When someone said to Yankees pitcher Lefty Gomez that Ferrell was temperamental, Gomez said, "I'd say he was 90 percent temperament and 10 percent mental."

Wes retired after 10 full seasons and parts of five others with a record of 193–128.

1. Name the Red Sox catcher (not on this list) who caught for a Red Sox championship team but also started for World Series winners for the Athletics and Yankees.

2. The Red Sox catcher who is the only player in history to hit into a triple play and then hit a grand slam his very next at bat is:
   a. Scott Hatteberg
   b. Gary Allenson
   c. Jim Pagliaroni
   d. Russ Gibson

3. Who is the catcher who took over as player-manager of the Red Sox and led them to a World Championship?

4. Who is one of only two players of all time to play in the Little League World Series, the College World Series, and the World Series?

5. In the first All-Star Game in 1933 this Sox catcher caught the entire game, even though Hall of Famers Bill Dickey and Mickey Cochrane were on the team.

6. Which catcher was selected for 11 All-Star Games? (Not all with the Red Sox)

7. Which catcher was selected for 7 All-Star Games in his career? (Not all with the Red Sox)

8. Name the Red Sox catcher who became both a professional bowler and a professional golfer after his baseball career ended.

9. Who set a record for putouts by a catcher in 1986 with 20 putouts, while catching Roger Clemens' 20 strikeouts?

10. Who was the catcher in Boston's first American League game? He also caught many of Cy Young's 511 career victories.

Answers

1. Wally Schang
2. a. Scott Hatteberg against the Texas Rangers in 2001
3. Bill Carrigan
4. Jason Varitek
5. Rick Ferrell
6. Carlton Fisk
7. Rick Ferrell
8. Sammy White
9. Rich Gedman
10. Lou Criger

Nine

Pitcher

The Rankings!

Starters

1. Cy Young
2. Roger Clemens
3. Pedro Martinez
4. Lefty Grove
5. Luis Tiant
6. Mel Parnell
7. "Smoky Joe" Wood
8. Babe Ruth
9. Carl Mays
10. Curt Schilling
11. Tim Wakefield
12. Jon Lester
13. Josh Beckett
14. Frank Sullivan
15. Bill Lee
16. Dutch Leonard
17. Dave "Boo" Ferris
18. Bill Monbouquette
19. Bruce Hurst
20. Tex Hughson
H.M. Dennis "Oil Can" Boyd
H.M. Jim Lonborg

Relievers

1. Dick Radatz
2. Jonathan Papelbon
3. Bob Stanley
4. Derek Lowe
5. Ellis Kinder
6. Tom Gordon
7. Jeff Reardon
8. Sparky Lyle
9. Bill Campbell
10. Lee Smith

The Rocket—Flushing, New York, 1986 *(Getty Images)*

The Red Sox pitching dominated baseball in the dead-ball era led by the legendary Cy Young, and then Joe Wood, who faded thanks to a sore arm after his fantastic 1912 season. Wood later became an outfielder with the Indians, just as Ruth did with the Yankees (in case you hadn't heard).

Grove was outstanding for some mediocre Red Sox teams in his post-A's days, while Parnell was the lefty mainstay after World War II. After that, only Tiant, Clemens, and Martinez would stay at the top of the Red Sox rotation for an extended period of time. Others would be an ace for a year or two and for various reasons would never reach those heights again. Though Schilling certainly made his mark on Red Sox history and Wakefield has been a rock for many years.

Among the relievers, many who saw him play still say Radatz is the best there ever was, but his career didn't last long enough for Hall of Fame consideration. Papelbon is the team's all-time saves leader. Stanley, Kinder, and Lowe were all longtime Sox favorites who both started and relieved. Lyle, Smith, and Reardon had longer tenures with—and more big years for—other clubs, while Gordon and Campbell had one year each at the top of the heap.

Before we take a look at some of the more interesting characters who've pitched for the Red Sox over the years, let's remember the stylish and gentlemanly left-hander who served as the team's ace for a decade in the late '40s and early '50s.

Mel Parnell

Mel Parnell won 20 games twice, led the league in wins with 25 in 1949, threw a no-hitter, and stands fourth on the team's all-time victory list with 123, well behind Roger Clemens, Cy Young, and Tim Wakefield.

His no-hitter, which came in 1956 against the White Sox at the end of his career, was the first no-hitter thrown by a Sox lefty since spitballer Dutch Leonard pitched a pair of no-hitters in 1918. And it would be the last by a Sox lefty until Jon Lester did the trick in 2008.

Parnell joined the Red Sox at the tail end of 1947, the year after they won the pennant, and in 1948 he posted a 15–8 record as the Sox came in second place, a game behind Cleveland. The next year was Parnell's best ever, as he finished 25–7 and led the league with a 3.34 ERA. Again the Sox lost the pennant, this time to the Yankees on the last day of the season. He won 18 games in each of the next two seasons and then slumped to 12–12 in 1952. But in '53 his record rebounded to 21–8 with a 3.06 ERA.

His career ended in 1956 because of a torn muscle in his pitching arm, but Parnell still holds the team's career record for left-handed pitchers in games started, innings pitched, and victories.

"I was different than most left-handers," Parnell said. "I pitched inside. If I could keep the ball in tight [then] they couldn't get their arms extended as much as they like to. That helped me at Fenway with the short left-field wall."

Parnell had a great slider that broke in at the last second. "I broke a lot of bats when I was pitching," he said. Parnell was particularly effective against two-time batting champion Ferris Fain. "He couldn't hit me with a tennis racquet. (Lou) Boudreau, (Harvey) Kuenn, and (Larry) Dobby were good contact hitters, and they were hard for me to get out. Mantle hit a few homers off me."

Parnell said that Casey Stengel didn't like him. "I was a low-ball pitcher and I wasn't giving the Yankees anything to hit," said Parnell. "In '53 he didn't take me to the All-Star Game because I beat the Yankees four times. My record was 12–4 at the All-Star break and he didn't take me. He didn't take me, Frank Larry, and Bob Porterfield because we beat him."

When his playing days were over, Parnell, a native Louisianan, managed the New Orleans Pelicans in Class Double AA and other Sox farm clubs, as well as working for the Red Sox as a TV and radio announcer from 1965–68.

Mel Parnell talked about some of his Red Sox teammates.

Ted Williams: "Ted was a good guy to get along with. The only problem was he would talk about hitting with opposing players and give them too much information that would help them."

"Williams was a great person to go to dinner with. He was smart, and the conversation was always lively. We had a lot of laughs.

"Ted was also a better fielder than he gets credit for being. He could play left field better than most guys. He may not have looked good making some plays because he was tall and gangly, but he'd get the ball."

Dom DiMaggio: "Dom was the best outfielder in baseball. I got a good view of him from the mound, and there was no one better. He was also a terrific person."

Vern Stephens: "He didn't get enough credit. He was a good right-handed power hitter and he loved Fenway."

Sammy White: "He was my catcher and we roomed together. He was the best catcher I had in my career. He gave the pitcher so much encouragement. He would tell me to just concern myself with throwing the ball. 'If I can't catch it, I can block it,' he would say. I would get him to call every pitch I had in the first inning, and at the end of the inning we'd talk and decide what was my "out" pitch that day."

Frank Sullivan: "He was a good pitcher and a good guy. He and Sammy were close, and they kept the clubhouse loose."

Mickey McDermott: "He was an entertainer. He could impersonate a lot of singers and he was pretty good. He had talent as a pitcher too, but he didn't take care of himself. He would have been great, but he never extended himself to use the ability he had. (Joe) McCarthy asked me to room with McDermott, to be like a father to the kid. Be like a father? I can't keep up with him."

Harry Agganis: "He was going to be a helluva player. You could see the ability in him. He was going to make it big. When Harry was ill Mr. Yawkey got him back to Boston. But we heard that the doctor knew Harry would never get out of the hospital. He was a good kid, and his death really upset us."

Ellis Kinder: "He was a good pitcher with great stuff and he knew how to use it. And he was a great competitor. He had the best change-up in baseball. But he had a bad drinking habit, and he didn't take his career seriously. He went out a lot. When he got on the mound he performed. When we fought the Yankees it was Kinder and me against Vic Raschi and Allie Reynolds. It was always a tough battle. Ellis was great both as a starter and as a reliever."

We've already talked about the Boston Red Sox Wes Ferrell, whose legendary temper was in the headlines throughout his very successful career. But Wes is only one in a long line of characters who somehow found their way onto the Red Sox staff.

After 110 years, there seems to be a pattern here. Here's a rundown of just some of the free spirits who've toiled on the hill for Boston.

Bill "Spaceman" Lee: The Spaceman was a solid Red Sox lefthander for a decade (1969–1978) who won 17 games three times and pitched in the 1975 World Series. Lee was a colorful guy who marched to the beat of his own drum. He came along as an outspoken counterculture, antiauthority figure who didn't hesitate to speak his mind about the issues of the day and also didn't hesitate to criticize management. He was loved by the writers who followed the team because he was always ready with a humorous quote.

When he was asked if he preferred grass or artificial turf, Spaceman replied, "I don't know. I never smoked the fake stuff."

Lee didn't have a great fastball, so he got by on guile. He had a variety of off-speed pitches, including his version of the high-arcing Eephus pitch, which he named the Leephus pitch or Space Ball. He began his career as a combination starter and reliever, but in 1973 he became a full-time starter, made the All-Star Game, and finished with a 17–11 record and a 2.95 ERA.

Lee had frequent run-ins with management, including an on-going feud with conservative manager Don Zimmer, whom Lee nicknamed the Gerbil.

Finally after the 1978 season, the Sox had had enough of the Spaceman's outspoken ways and sent him off to Montreal, where he had one more big season with a 16–4 record. He finished his career with a lifetime 119–90 record.

Lee, who holds the Red Sox record for most games pitched by a left-hander, was inducted into the Red Sox Hall of Fame in 2008.

Gene Conley: This two-sport star from Washington State is the only man in history to win a World Series and an NBA championship.

The 6'8" pitcher worked in the majors for 11 seasons, made the All-Star game twice, and made a brief appearance in the 1957 World Series for the eventual champion Milwaukee Braves. He was also Bill Russell's backup on the Boston Celtics championship squads of 1958–59 and 1959–60, later going on to play for the Knicks.

The incident that Conley is best remembered for, though, took place in 1961, when he was a member of the Red Sox. It was in New York, and the Yankees clobbered Conley in an 11–3 slaughter. Conley left the game and spent the rest of the afternoon drinking beer in the clubhouse. He was pretty well lit later that day when the Sox bus got bogged down in a traffic jam on the way to the airport for a trip to Washington. Conley and teammate Pumpsie Green got off the bus, and that was the last anyone saw of them for a while. Pumpsie turned up the next day, but Conley was gone for three whole days.

He reportedly tried to get a trip to Jerusalem, but he didn't have a passport, so he just went to a hotel and watched TV for three days while everyone was looking for him.

Conley was embarrassed and contrite when he did return, and he settled down and did pretty well for the remainder of the season.

Jonathan Papelbon: The Red Sox closer for the past five years—and 2011 is probably his last in Boston, as he'll be a free agent—embraces has reputation as a flake.

Papelbon, the all-time Sox save leader, is another standout pitcher who does everything with a little pizzazz, from the Mohawk to the stare to his choreography on the mound. Papelbon listens to the voices in his head that tell him to go out and have fun. For the past five years Papelbon has given the Sox a steady, consistent relief ace, and in three of those seasons he's helped them in the postseason.

But 2011 is Papelbon's contract year, and the combination of some 2010 lapses mixed with up-and-comers like Daniel Bard make it unlikely that the 30-year-old hurler will get his big payoff from the Red Sox.

Papelbon served as the Sox closer for most of the 2006 season and was expected to be a starter the following year. However, he suffered shoulder problems and eventually moved back to the bullpen where he became the team's first-ever back-to-back 30-save man. He was also the first pitcher to save 30 games in every one of his first five major league seasons.

In 2007, Papelbon celebrated the Sox clinching of the AL East title by doing an Irish victory dance on the infield at Fenway Park as the PA blared Dropkick Murphys' "I'm Shipping Up to Boston," which is the song that plays as Papelbon enters a game. He repeated the dance on the field with some of the band members from Dropkick Murphys after the team won the American League pennant, and did it again holding the World Series Trophy over his head on the flatbed truck during the victory parade.

In 2009 Papelbon earned his 133rd save with the Red Sox to pass Bob Stanley as the all-time save leader.

Dennis "Oil Can" Boyd: A pretty good starter for the Sox in the '80s, the flamboyant Oil Can was burdened by a temperament similar to that of the angry Wes Ferrell. He was cocky, moody, and high-strung; and that held him back from living up to his vast potential and made him a not-too-popular figure in the clubhouse. He did have a few good years, winning 15 and 16 in 1985 and '86,

One of the dominant pitchers of the pro-offense, modern era, Pedro fires another fastball at the Yankees.

respectively, but he went ballistic when he wasn't chosen for the All-Star Game either year. The Red Sox suspended him in '86, and he checked into a hospital to help with his emotional problems. Later he was bothered by blood clots in his right shoulder that limited his effectiveness.

A colorful character who was always good for a quote, it was Boyd who said, after fog caused the postponement of a game in Cleveland, "That's what they get for building a park on the ocean."

That's just a sampling of the Red Sox characters who've made life interesting at Fenway.

Others, such as Roger Clemens, Pedro Martinez, Luis Tiant, Ellis Kinder, and of course Babe Ruth also brought their own flaws, eccentricities, foibles, and odd behavior to the game.

Match the Red Sox pitcher with the year he won 20 games.

1.	Tex Hughson	a.	2004
2.	Josh Beckett	b.	1935
3.	Lefty Grove	c.	1978
4.	Babe Ruth	d.	1912
5.	Curt Schilling	e.	1944
6.	Bill Monbouquette	f.	2007
7.	"Sad Sam" Jones	g.	1967
8.	Dennis Eckersley	h.	1916
9.	Jim Lonborg	i.	1963
10.	"Smoky Joe" Wood	j.	1921

Answers
1. e
2. f
3. b
4. h
5. a
6. i
7. j
8. c
9. g
10. d

Ten

The Greats

"They can talk about Babe Ruth and Ty Cobb and
Rogers Hornsby and Lou Gehrig and Joe DiMaggio
and Stan Musial and all the rest, but I'm sure not one
of them could hold cards and spades to Williams in his
sheer knowledge of hitting. He studied hitting the way
a broker studies the stock market, and could spot at a
glance mistakes that others couldn't see in a week."

—Carl Yastrzemski

The Ted Williams Quiz

1. In 1941, the year that Ted Williams hit .406, making him the last major leaguer to hit .400, who finished with the second-highest batting average in the American League?
   a. Joe DiMaggio
   b. Cecil Travis
   c. Bobby Doerr
   d. Hank Greenberg

2. Name the pitcher who served up Ted's final home run on September 28, 1960.

3. Who pinch-hit for Ted in his next scheduled at bat in that game?
   a. Marty Keough
   b. Gary Geiger
   c. Lu Clinton
   d. Carroll Hardy

4. In what two years did Ted Williams win the AL Triple Crown?

5. Which of the following was NOT one of Ted Williams' nicknames?
   a. Teddy Ballgame
   b. The Boston Belter
   c. The Splendid Splinter
   d. Thumper

6. How many times, and in what years, did Ted hit 40 home runs or more?

7. Who was the Red Sox starting left fielder before Williams took over in 1940?

8. In what two years did Williams win the AL Most Valuable Player Award?

9. What was the only year in which Ted Williams played in the World Series?

10. In 1956, Ted Williams hit the last of his four career All-Star game home runs. Name the National League pitcher who gave up that four-bagger.

Answers

1. b. Cecil Travis of the Senators hit .359. Joe DiMaggio was third with .357 in the year of his 56-game hitting streak.
2. Jack Fisher of the Orioles
3. d. Carroll Hardy
4. 1942 and 1947
5. b. The Boston Belter
6. One time, 1949
7. Joe Vosmik
8. 1946 and 1949
9. 1946
10. Warren Spahn

The Carl Yastrzemski Quiz

1. In 1967 Yaz won the AL Triple Crown with a .326 average. Who was second in batting average that year at .311?
   a. Frank Robinson
   b. Al Kaline
   c. Tony Oliva
   d. Rod Carew
2. Yaz won the 1967 RBI crown with 121. Who was the only other AL player to have more than 100 RBIs that year?
3. In 1967, a Red Sox pitcher and teammate of Yastrzemski tied for the AL co-lead in victories with 22. Who was this Red Sox hurler, and what pitcher did he tie with?
4. Name the other two starting outfielders in the Red Sox lineup that year.
5. Which National League pitcher was on the mound in 1975 when Yaz hit his only All-Star Game home run?
6. How many times did Yaz reach the 40–home run mark?
7. In what two years other than 1967 did he win the AL batting crown?
8. What was Yastrzemski's lifetime batting average?
9. How many Gold Gloves did Yaz win?
10. When Yaz was called up to the Red Sox to start in 1961, the Sox had another rookie starting at second base. Who was he?

Answers

1. a. Frank Robinson
2. Harmon Killebrew, with 113.
3. Jim Lonborg and Earl Wilson of the Tigers
4. Reggie Smith in center field and Tony Conigliaro in right field.
5. Tom Seaver
6. Three times. He hit 44 in 1967, and 40 in both 1969 and 1970.
7. In 1963 he won with a .321 average and in 1968 with a .301 average.
8. .285
9. Seven
10. Chuck Schilling

The Jim Rice Quiz

1. Which National League pitcher was on the mound when Jim Rice hit a home run in the 1983 All-Star Game?

2. How many times, and in what years, did Jim Rice lead the American League in home runs?

3. How many times did the Red Sox go to the playoffs during Jim Rice's career, and in what years?

4. Who were Rice's outfield mates in the mid and late '70s?

5. In what year did Jim Rice win the AL MVP Award?

6. Who finished second in the voting that year?

7. How many times was Jim Rice selected for the AL All-Star team?

8. What was Rice's career batting average?

9. True or False? Jim Rice once led the American League in triples.

10. In 1977, Rice led the AL with 39 home runs. Name the two other Red Sox who had at least 30 homers that year.

Answers

1. Atlee Hammaker
2. Three. In 1977 he hit 39, in 1978 he hit 46, and in 1983 he hit 39.
3. Twice. In 1986 and 1988.
4. Fred Lynn in center and Dwight Evans in right.
5. 1978
6. Ron Guidry, pitcher for the Yankees
7. Eight times
8. .298
9. True. He led the AL with 15 triples in 1978. He also hit 15 the previous year, but Rod Carew had 16.
10. George Scott hit 33 homers and Butch Hobson hit 30.

The Carlton Fisk Quiz

1. Off which Cincinnati Reds pitcher did Fisk hit his famous 12th-inning, walk-off home run in the 1975 World Series?
2. Name the Yankees catcher with whom Fisk feuded. They got into a bench-clearing brawl in 1973 and were both ejected from the game.
3. Another bench-clearing brawl in 1976 that started with a fight between Fisk and Lou Piniella of the Yankees resulted in which Red Sox pitcher suffering a separated shoulder?
4. In 1985 as a member of the White Sox, Fisk tagged out two Yankees at home plate on the same play. Who were they?
5. Who was the shortstop who took the throw from the outfield and relayed it to Fisk at home plate for the double tag?
6. In 1990, Fisk hit his 328th career home run, breaking whose record for homers by a catcher?
7. In 1984, Fisk hit for the cycle with a 7th-inning triple off what Royals pitcher?
8. What two awards did Carlton Fisk win in 1972?
9. In 1986, Fisk caught the 300th victory for which Hall of Fame pitcher?
10. In 1993, Fisk caught his 2,226th game in the majors to break a record set by which catcher?

Answers

1. Pat Darcy
2. Thurman Munson
3. Bill Lee
4. Bobby Meacham and Dale Berra
5. Ozzie Guillen
6. Johnny Bench. This record has since been broken by Mike Piazza, but Fisk still holds the American League record.
7. Dan Quisenberry
8. The Gold Glove and the AL Rookie of the Year
9. Tom Seaver
10. Bob Boone. The record has since been broken by Ivan Rodríguez.

The Nomar Garciaparra Quiz

1. Name the international soccer star who is Mrs. Nomar Garciaparra.
2. Name the three teams Nomar played for after leaving the Red Sox in 2004.
3. Nomar played in the College World Series for which college?
4. Who was the Boston shortstop who moved to second base when Garciaparra won the shortstop job?
5. Who was the *Saturday Night Live* comedian whose character in a recurring skit "The Boston Teens" idolized "No-mah," which he pronounced with a thick Boston accent?
6. In 1997, Garciaparra won the AL Rookie of the Year Award. Who won the National League award?
7. The highest Nomar ever finished in the MVP voting was second, in 1998. Who won the AL MVP that year?
8. Nomar was selected for his first All-Star Game in 1997, but who was the AL's starting shortstop that year?
9. What was Nomar's highest one-season batting average in his career, and in what year was it accomplished?
10. When Nomar hit two grand slams in one game he tied a record that he now shares with three other Red Sox. Name one of these record holders.

Answers

1. Mia Hamm
2. The Chicago Cubs (2004–2005), the Los Angeles Dodgers (2006–2008), and the Oakland Athletics (2009)
3. Georgia Tech
4. John Valentin
5. Jimmy Fallon
6. Scott Rolen of the Phillies
7. Juan Gonzalez of the Texas Rangers
8. Cal Ripken, Jr.
9. He hit .372 in 2000.
10. Jim Tabor in 1939, Rudy York in 1946, and Bill Mueller in 2003.

Eleven

Potpourri

The Red Sox College All-Star Basketball Team

You could put together a pretty fair basketball team with former Red Sox players. The requirement we went with in making our list was that the player had to be at least a starter on a major college team, though many of these players were outright stars. We've included some information about each player's basketball career and a note on the years he played for the Red Sox.

F Jerry Mallett (Baylor) 6'5", Red Sox 1959: Honorable Mention All-American and three-time All Southwest Conference, drafted by the NBA's Syracuse Nationals.

F Garry Roggenburk (Dayton) 6'6", Red Sox 1967–1969: All-American led Flyers to NIT championship in 1962, drafted by the San Francisco Warriors.

F Walt Dropo (UCONN) 6'5", Red Sox 1949–1952: Was the leading career scorer when he graduated from UCONN. AL Rookie of the Year with the Sox in 1950. Drafted by basketball's Providence Steamrollers.

F Don Schwall (Oklahoma) 6'6", Red Sox 1961–1962: All-Big Eight for the Sooners in 1957 and AL Rookie of the Year with the Sox in 1961.

F Dave Sisler (Princeton) 6'4", Red Sox 1956–1959: All-Ivy League and member of Princeton NCAA team.

C Gene Conley (Washington State and NBA) 6'8", Red Sox 1961–1963: Honorable Mention All-American two years. Only player to win a World Series and an NBA title, doing so with the Milwaukee Braves and Boston Celtics.

C Ron Jackson (Western Michigan) 6'7", Red Sox 1960: Set career rebounding record for Western Michigan and was named All-Mid American Conference two years.

C Tony Clark (Arizona and San Diego State) 6'8", Red Sox 2002: Starter for Arizona and San Diego State, led Aztecs in scoring his senior year.

G Jerry Adair (Oklahoma State) 6'1", Red Sox 1967–1968: Second-leading scorer for Oklahoma State on a team that went to the NCAA regional final.

G Sam Mele (NYU) 6'1", Red Sox 1947–1949, 1954–1955: He was the top scorer for NYU in the early '40s. He's the only person to lead his college team in scoring in the NCAA Tournament (18 PPG in 1943) and lead the American League in doubles (36 for the 1961 Senators).

G Billy Werber (Duke) 5'10", Red Sox 1933–1936: All-American at Duke, three-time stolen base champion and a member of Reds World Series teams in 1939 and 1940.

G Sonny Siebert (Missouri) 6'3", Red Sox 1969–1973: Leading scorer at Mizzou and a draft pick of the St. Louis Hawks.

G Sammy White (Washington) 6'3", Red Sox 1951–1959: All-Pacific Coast Conference in basketball while leading the Huskies to

Carl Yastrzemski on the cover of *LIFE.* *(Getty Images)*

the NCAA tournament in 1948. He spurned an offer to play for the Minneapolis Lakers in order to pursue his baseball career.

G Lou Boudreau (Illinois) 5'11", with the Red Sox as a player and/or manager 1951–1954: Hall of Fame shortstop played most of his 15-year playing career with the Indians. Boudreau was an All-American for the University of Illinois and played professionally with the Hammond All-Americans of the National Basketball League.

We also have the makings of a pretty good college football team starting with Jackie Jensen, an All-American running back at Cal, Harry Agganis of Boston University, Carroll Hardy, from Colorado, who played defensive back for the 49ers, and Galen Cisco, a star at Ohio State.

New York Red Sox

We hate to do this to you Boston, but this is an All-Red Sox team of players who hail from the New York metropolitan area. This is just a good-natured reminder to Boston fans about the great debt they owe to New York. We realize that this is a team centered around Yaz, Petro, Malzy, Manny, Valentin, and Stanley, and everyone else is a relatively short-term Sox player (except Heinie Wagner, but he's a little past his prime). But that's a pretty good nucleus.

Starting Lineup and Years Played for the Sox
First Base: Joe Judge, 1933–1934
Second Base: Heinie Wagner, 1906–1916
Shortstop: Rico Petrocelli, 1963–1976
Third Base: Frank Malzone, 1955–1966
Outfield: Manny Ramirez, 2001–2008 (Born in the Dominican Republic, grew up in New York);
Carl Yastrzemski, 1961–1983 (Hall of Fame); and
Sam Mele, 1947–1949, 1954–1955

Catcher: Rick Cerone, 1988–1989
Designated Hitter: John Valentin, 1992–2001
Starting pitchers: Waite Hoyt, 1919–1920 (Hall of Fame)
Frank Viola, 1992–1994
Mike Nagy, 1969–1972
Milt Gaston, 1929–1931
Dick Brodowski, 1952, 1955
Jerry Casale, 1958–1960
Ken Brett, 1967, 1969–1971
Relievers: Bob Stanley, 1977-1989
Johnny Murphy, 1947
Joey Sambito, 1986–1987
Don McMahon, 1966–1967
Hank Fischer, 1966–1967
Jack Lamabe, 1963–1965
Heathcliff Slocumb, 1996–1997
Leo Kiely, 1951, 1954–1959

Reserves
Catchers: Moe Berg, 1935–1939 and Joe Ginsberg, 1961
Infielders: Eddie Kasko, 1966; Ken Aspromonte, 1957–1958; Joe Foy, 1966–1968; and Chuck Schilling, 1961–1965
Outfielder: Hack Miller, 1916–1918

The mighty Jim Rice puts a hurtin' on another ball. *(Getty Images)*

The All-Red Sox Managers Team and Years Served as Manager in Boston

First Base: Frank Chance* (1923) Honorable Mention: Rudy York (1959) and Pete Runnels (1966)

Second Base: Billy Herman* (1964–1966) Honorable Mention: Heinie Wagner (1930) and Bucky Harris* (1934)

Shortstop: Joe Cronin* (1935–1947) Honorable Mention: Lou Boudreau* (1952–1954); Johnny Pesky (1963–1964, 1980); Billy Jurges (1959–1960); Don Zimmer (1976–1980); and Jack Barry (1917)

Third Base: Jimmy Collins* (1901–1906) Honorable Mention: Marty McManus (1932–1933); Mike "Pinky" Higgins (1955–1959, 1960–1962); and Butch Hobson (1992–1994)

Outfield: Hugh Duffy* (1921–1922), Chick Stahl (1906), and Patsy Donovan (1910–1911) Honorable Mention: Jake Stahl (1912–1913), Shano Collins (1931–1932), Dick Williams* (1997–2001), and Terry Francona (2004 to present)

Catcher: Deacon McGuire (1907–1908) Honorable Mention: Bill Carrigan (1913–1916, 1927–1929) and Steve O'Neill (1950–1951)

Pitcher: Cy Young* (1908) Honorable Mention: Joe Kerrigan (2001)

*Hall of Famer

Twelve

Honors

Red Sox Inducted into the Hall of Fame

First Base: Jimmie Foxx, Tony Perez, and Orlando Cepeda
Second Base: Bobby Doerr
Shortstop: Joe Cronin, Lou Boudreau, and Luis Aparicio
Third Base: Jimmy Collins, Wade Boggs, and George Kell
Outfield: Ted Williams, Carl Yastrzemski, Jim Rice, Tris Speaker, Harry Hooper, Jesse Burkett, Rickey Henderson, Al Simmons, and Heinie Manush
Catcher: Carlton Fisk and Rick Ferrell
Pitcher: Babe Ruth, Cy Young, Jack Chesbro, Lefty Grove, Dennis Eckersley, Ferguson Jenkins, Juan Marichal, Waite Hoyt, Red Ruffing, Herb Pennock, and Tom Seaver
Manager: Dick Williams

Red Sox Who Made AL All-Star Team at Least Four Times While a Member of the Red Sox

First Base: Jimmie Foxx (6) and David Ortiz (5)
Second Base: Bobby Doerr (9)
Shortstop: Joe Cronin (7), Nomar Garciaparra (5), and Vern Stephens (4)

Third Base: Wade Boggs (8) and Frank Malzone (6)
Outfield: Ted Williams (16), Carl Yastrzemski (18), Dom DiMaggio (7), Fred Lynn (6), Doc Cramer (4), Manny Ramirez (7), and Jim Rice (8)
Catcher: Carlton Fisk (7) and Rick Ferrell (4)
Pitcher: Roger Clemens (5), Lefty Grove (5), Pedro Martinez (4), and Dick Radatz (7)

* The All-Star Game began in 1933, which is why early 20th century players such as Cy Young, Tris Speaker, Harry Hooper, and others do not appear on this list.

*There were two All-Star Games in the years 1959 to 1962, but they will count as one selection each for the purposes of this list.

Red Sox Cited on MLB Network's *Prime 9*

Prime 9 is a countdown show by MLB Productions for MLB Network ranking the all-time top nine in a variety of categories. *Prime 9* is designed to start arguments, not end them. Here is a list of Red Sox who made the "top 9" on various shows and where they were ranked.

Top 9 Third Basemen
No. 5: Wade Boggs

Top 9 All-Star Moments
No. 2: Ted Williams' walk-off home run in 1941

Top 9 Greatest Comebacks
No. 1: 2004 Red Sox comeback from 0–3 against the Yankees to win AL pennant
   The Red Sox trailed the Yankees three games to zero in the bottom of the ninth, when Bill Mueller's single scored Dave Roberts to tie the score and send the game into extra innings. In the bottom

of the 12th David Ortiz's walk-off home run with Manny Ramirez aboard won the game 6–4. The Sox went on to win the next three games and beat the Yankees 4–3 for the AL pennant. Boston went on to a 4–0 sweep of the Cardinals in the World Series.

No. 4: Red Sox in Game 5 of the 1986 ALCS

The Sox were trailing 5–2 going into the 9th inning against the Angels. Boston scored four runs in the top of the ninth to make it 6–5. The Angels scored in the bottom of the ninth to tie the game at 6–6 and send it into extra innings. In the top of the 11th Dave Henderson's sacrifice fly scored Don Baylor for what turned out to be the winning run.

Top 9 Baseball Gaffes

No. 1: Bill Buckner letting the ball go through his legs against the Mets in the 1986 World Series

Top 9 Greatest Pitching Seasons

No. 1: Pedro Martinez, 2000

Martinez was 18–6 and led the league with a 1.74 ERA with 4 shutouts and also led with 284 strikeouts, while giving up only 32 walks and 128 hits in 217 innings on the way to this third Cy Young Award. Considering the era in which he did this, it's pretty unbelievable.

Top 9 Home Runs

No. 7: Carlton Fisk's homer in the 1975 World Series

Top 9 Clutch Hitters

No. 4: David Ortiz

Top 9 Closers

No. 5: Dennis Eckersley

No. 8: Lee Smith (Both played for the Red Sox but had their best seasons as closers with the A's and Cubs, respectively.)

Top 9 Catchers
No. 5: Carlton Fisk

Top 9 Unique Pitching Deliveries
No. 1: Luis Tiant (No. 2: Juan Marichal pitched for the Red Sox in 1974)

Top 9 Outfield Arms
No. 8: Dwight Evans

Top 9 Trades
No. 1: Babe Ruth from the Red Sox to the Yankees for $125,000 in 1919.
No. 4: Jason Varitek and Derek Lowe from the Mariners for Heathcliff Slocumb in 1997.

Top 9 Left Fielders
No. 1: Ted Williams
No. 5: Manny Ramirez
No. 8: Carl Yastrzemski

Top 9 Designated Hitters
No. 3: David Ortiz
No. 7: Don Baylor (with the Sox in 1986 and 1987)

The All-1960s Team
No. 6: LF Carl Yastrzemski

Players of the '80s
No. 9: RF Dwight Evans

Top 9 Team Broadcasters
No. 9: Curt Gowdy, Red Sox (1951–1966)

Top 9 Greatest Ballparks
No. 2: Fenway Park

Red Sox Awards
Triple Crown: Batting
Ted Williams, (2) 1942, 1947
Carl Yastrzemski, 1967

MVP
Ted Williams, (2) 1946, 1949
Jimmie Foxx, 1938
Jackie Jensen, 1958
Carl Yastrzemski, 1967
Fred Lynn, 1975
Jim Rice, 1978
Roger Clemens, 1986
Mo Vaughn, 1995
Dustin Pedroia, 2008

Cy Young Award
Roger Clemens, (3) 1986, 1987, 1991
Pedro Martinez, (2) 1999, 2000
Jim Lonborg, 1967

Rookie of the Year
Walt Dropo, 1950
Don Schwall, 1961
Carlton Fisk, 1972
Fred Lynn, 1975
Nomar Garciaparra, 1997
Dustin Pedroia, 2007

Batting Champions
Ted Williams, (6) 1941, 1942, 1947, 1948, 1957, 1958
Wade Boggs, (5) 1983, 1985, 1986, 1987, 1988
Carl Yastrzemski, (3) 1963, 1967, 1968
Pete Runnels, (2) 1960, 1962
Nomar Garciaparra, (2) 1999, 2000
Tris Speaker, 1916
Dale Alexander, 1932
Jimmie Foxx, 1938
Billy Goodman, 1950
Fred Lynn, 1979
Carney Lansford, 1981
Manny Ramirez, 2002
Bill Mueller, 2003

Triple Crown: Pitching
(Wins, ERA, Strikeouts)
Cy Young, 1901
Pedro Martinez, 1999

Home Run Champions
Ted Williams, (4) 1941, 1942, 1947, 1949
Jim Rice, (3) 1977, 1978, 1983
Tony Conigliaro, 1965
Dwight Evans, 1981
Tony Armas, 1984

ERA Champions
Lefty Grove, (4) 1935, 1936, 1938, 1939
Roger Clemens, (4) 1986, 1990, 1991, 1992
Pedro Martinez, (3) 1999, 2000, 2002
Cy Young, 1901

Dutch Leonard, 1914
Joe Wood, 1915
Babe Ruth, 1915
Mel Parnell, 1949
Luis Tiant, 1972

Strikeout Champions
Roger Clemens, (3) 1988, 1991, 1996
Pedro Martinez, (3) 1999, 2000, 2002
Cy Young, 1901
Tex Hughson, 1942
Jim Lonborg, 1967
Hideo Nomo, 2001

Boston Red Sox Hall of Fame

First Base: Jimmie Foxx (1995), Pete Runnels (2004), George Scott (2006), and Mo Vaughn (2008)
Second Base: Bobby Doerr (1995), Billy Goodman (2004), and Jerry Remy (2006)
Shortstop: Rick Burleson (2002), Joe Cronin (1995), Johnny Pesky (1995), Rico Petrocelli (1997), Everett Scott (2008), Vern Stephens (2006), and John Valentin (2010)
Third Base: Wade Boggs (2004), Jimmy Collins, Manager (1995), Larry Gardner (2000), and Frank Malzone (1995)
Outfield: Tony Conigliaro (1995), Dom DiMaggio (1995), Dwight Evans (2000), Mike Greenwell (2008), Tommy Harper (2010), Harry Hooper (1995), Jackie Jensen (2000), Duffy Lewis (2002), Fred Lynn (2002), Jimmy Piersall, (2010), Jim Rice (1995), Reggie Smith (2000), Tris Speaker (1995), Ted Williams (1995), and Carl Yastrzemski (1995),
Catcher: Bill Carrigan, Manager (2004), Rick Ferrell (1995), and Carlton Fisk (1997)

Pitcher: Dennis Eckersley (2004), Wes Ferrell (2008), Dave "Boo" Ferris (2002), Lefty Grove (1995), Cecil "Tex" Hughson (2002), Bruce Hurst (2004), Ellis Kinder (2006), Bill Lee (2008), Jim Lonborg (2002), Bill Monbouquette (2000), Mel Parnell (1997), Herb Pennock (1995), Dick Radatz (1997), Babe Ruth (1995), Bob Stanley (2000), Frank Sullivan (2008), Luis Tiant (1997), Smoky Joe Wood (1995), and Cy Young (1995)
Manager: Joe Morgan (2006), Dick Williams (2006), and Don Zimmer (2010)
Executive: Dick Bresciani (2006), Eddie Collins (1995), George Digby, Scout (2008), Lou Gorman (2002), John Harrington (2002), Eddie Kasko, Scout (2010), Ed Kennedy, Sr. (2008), Ben Mondor, PawSox Executive (2004), Dick O'Connell (1997), Heywood Sullivan (2004), Jean Yawkey, Owner (1995), and Tom Yawkey, Owner (1995)
Broadcaster: Curt Gowdy (2000), John Harrington (2002), and Ned Martin (2000)

Annual Awards
These awards were presented at the Boston Chapter of the BBWAA and Sports Museum at their 72nd Annual Dinner in January 2011.

The Emil Fuchs Award for Long and Meritorious Service to Baseball: Larry Lucchino
The Yawkey Award for the Red Sox MVP: Adrian Beltre
Red Sox Pitcher of the Year: Jon Lester, Clay Buchholz
Red Sox Fireman of the Year: Daniel Bard
The Jackie Jensen Hustle Award: Darnell McDonald
The Good Guy Award: Bill Hall
The Unsung Hero Award: Scott Atchison
The Red Sox Comeback Player of the Year Award: Jed Lowrie

The Harry Agganis Award for the Red Sox Rookie of the Year:
Ryan Kalish
The Greg Montalbano Memorial Minor League Award: Anthony
Rizzo
The Dave O'Hara Lifetime Award for Baseball Writing: Mike Shalin
The Community Service Award: Tim Wakefield
**The Ben Mondor Memorial Award for New England Player of the
Year:** Carl Pavano, Twins
The Tony Conigliaro MLB Comeback Award: Joaquin Benoit of the
Rays (later with the Tigers)
The Ted Williams Award for AL MVP: Josh Hamilton, Rangers
The Manager of the Year: Ron Washington, Rangers
Executive of the Year: Brian Sabean, Giants
Special Achievement Awards: Umpire Jim Joyce and Tigers
pitcher Armando Galarraga
Special Achievement Award: Mike Lowell
Former Red Sox Award: Dennis "Oil Can" Boyd

The Hitters Hall of Fame at the Ted Williams Museum

The 20 baseball legends that follow were chosen by Ted Williams
as the greatest hitters of all time, and were honored in 1995 as the
first class of the Hitters Hall of Fame at the Ted Williams Museum at
Tropicana Field in St. Petersburg, Florida.

Each of these inductees has a display case in the museum
featuring memorabilia and photos to commemorate the player's
career.

Ted's 20 Greatest Hitters of All Time
Babe Ruth
Ty Cobb
Hank Greenberg
Mel Ott

Lou Gehrig
Stan Musial
Mickey Mantle
Harry Heilmann
Jimmie Foxx
Joe Jackson
Tris Speaker
Frank Robinson
Rogers Hornsby
Hank Aaron
Al Simmons
Mike Schmidt
Joe DiMaggio
Willie Mays
Johnny Mize
Ralph Kiner

Those inducted since that first class in 1995
Roberto Alomar, 2007
Ernie Banks, 1998
Johnny Bench, 2000
Yogi Berra, 1999
Wade Boggs, 2003
George Brett, 2000
Rod Carew, 2004
Will Clark, 2009
Roberto Clemente, 2000
Andre Dawson, 2007
Dom DiMaggio, 2003
Brian Downing, 2010
Dwight Evans, 2002

Carlton Fisk, 2000
Josh Gibson, 1996
Tony Gwynn, 2003
Monte Irvin, 2004
Reggie Jackson, 1998
Al Kaline, 1999
Harmon Killebrew, 1996
Chuck Klein, 1996
Buck Leonard, 1998
Roger Maris, 2002
Eddie Mathews, 1998
Don Mattingly, 2002
Willie McCovey, 1996
Fred McGriff, 2006
Paul Molitor, 2001
Dale Murphy, 2006
Sadaharu Oh, 1999
Jim Rice, 2001
Cal Ripken Jr., 2002
Pete Rose, 2003
Enos Slaughter, 2002
Duke Snider, 1996
Willie Stargell, 1999
Darryl Strawberry, 2009
Ted Williams, 2003
Dave Winfield, 2001
Carl Yastrzemski, 1999
Robin Yount, 2001

Thirteen

Quotes By and About the Red Sox

"When Ted Williams took batting practice we stopped and watched him. He was the greatest hitter I ever saw."

— Bill "Moose" Skowron, New York Yankees

"We were down 0–3 to the Yankees when we decided to do it, but we did it. And we shocked the world."

—Johnny Damon

"Fred Lynn is the most complete player in our league. But when you think of the most dangerous hitter, you think of a [Jim] Rice or [Don] Baylor, a guy who scares you every time he comes to the plate."

—Toronto manager Roy Hartsfield, 1979

"I'm gaining weight the right way: I'm drinking beer."

—Johnny Damon

"I'm in the twilight of a mediocre career."

—Frank Sullivan, when he was with the Twins

"Some guys didn't like to lose, but Rick (Burleson) got angry if the score was even tied."

—Bill "Spaceman" Lee

"You can be in the league your whole career and never make it to a World Series. For me to do it in my first year and be part of a World Series championship team is very special."

—Jacoby Ellsbury

"He could speak in eight languages, but he couldn't hit in any of them."

—White Sox pitcher Ted Lyons about catcher Moe Berg

"I swing hard all the time. That's what I've done my whole life—hit."

—David Ortiz

"Dick Radatz brings one weapon—a fastball. It's like saying all a country brings to a war is an atom bomb."

—Jim Murray, sportswriter

"We are just 'the idiots' this year."

—Johnny Damon, 2004

"We're just being ourselves and having fun playing baseball. The biggest thing is when people look at our team, they can see that we're having a lot of fun."

—Johnny Damon

"I think if you come to the ballpark and you see Carl (Crawford) hit a triple, you've had a pretty good day. It's pretty much a signature play for him. Because when he hits the ball down the line, or in the gap, he's thinking three. He never thinks two. He breaks [for a] triple. He wants triple, he takes triple."

— Rays manager Joe Maddon

"I think Bobby Doerr could turn the double play better than anyone alive."

—Mel Parnell

"Whatever criticism you may make about (Carl) Mays, he has more guts than any pitcher I ever saw."

—Everett Scott

"The difference between us and the Yankees in 1949 was that we didn't have a guy like Joe Page in our bullpen. He could have made the difference on our team."

—Mel Parnell

"[He is] a smart, shrewd ballplayer, always working for the best interests of his club, and an inspiration to his fellow players."
        —*Sporting News*, February 1, 1923, about Larry Gardner

"One time I was in a slump, and when I went to Boston, I asked Ted [Williams] what I was doing wrong. He said, 'You're trying to pull the ball too much. Try to hit the opposite way.' I took his advice and hit two home runs into the bullpen in right center. After the game, Ted called me and asked me not to tell anyone what he said."

—Bill "Moose" Skowron

"They asked me about mandatory drug testing. I said I believed in drug testing a long time ago. All through the '60s I tested everything!"

—Bill "Spaceman" Lee

"The reason he (Earl Webb) hits so many doubles is that he hits a long, hard ball, and he's too darned slow on the bases to get to third."

—Red Sox manager Shano Collins

"Can I throw harder than Joe Wood? Listen, my friend, there's no man alive can throw harder than 'Smoky Joe' Wood."

—Walter Johnson

"I usually play a short field because I believe it is a decided advantage to do so. But of course in the case of such a batter as Pipp, it would be foolish to play in. You have to go way back for those sluggers."

—Tris Speaker

"Spread the diaper in the position of the diamond with you at bat. Then, fold second base down to home and set the baby on the pitcher's mound. Put first base and third together, bring up home plate, and pin the three together. Of course, in case of rain, you gotta call the game and start all over again."

— Jimmy Piersall, on how to diaper a baby

"Baseball is the only field of endeavor where a man can succeed three times out of ten and be considered a good performer."

—Ted Williams

"By the time you know what to do, you're too old to do it."

—Ted Williams

"If there was ever a man born to be a hitter it was me."

—Ted Williams

"I hope somebody hits .400 soon. Then people can start pestering that guy with questions about the last guy to hit .400."

—Ted Williams

"One of the fellows called me 'Cyclone' but finally shortened it to 'Cy' and it's been that ever since."

—Cy Young

"When I was a rookie, Cy Young used to hit me flies to sharpen my abilities to judge in advance the direction and distance of an outfield-hit ball."

—Tris Speaker

"Johnny Pesky goes, 'Ted Williams was the greatest hitter of all time.' He says that over and over and over. Now it's to a point where I'll say, 'Johnny, I have to ask you a question: who the hell is Ted Williams?' I just like messing with him."

—Dustin Pedroia

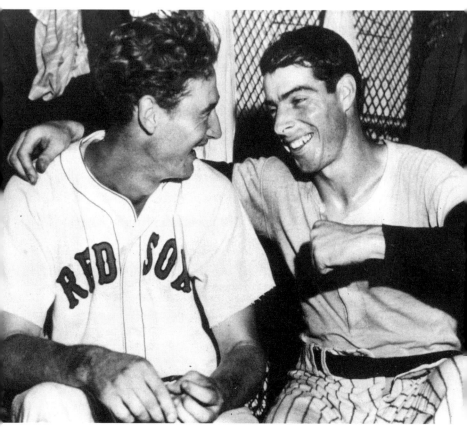

Joe DiMaggio congratulates Ted Williams on his 9th-inning home run, which sent the AL to a 7–5 victory in the 1941 All-Star Game.

"Joe DiMaggio was the greatest all-around player I ever saw. His career cannot be summed up in numbers and awards. It might sound corny, but he had a profound and lasting impact on the country."

—Ted Williams

"Babe Ruth made a grave mistake when he gave up pitching. Working once a week he might have lasted a long time and become a great star."

—Tris Speaker

"An outfield composed of Ty Cobb, Tris Speaker, and Babe Ruth, even with Ruth, lacks the combined power of [Joe] DiMaggio, [Stan] Musial, and [Ted] Williams."

—Connie Mack

"Ty Cobb would have to play center field on my all-time team. But where would that put Speaker? In left. If I had them both, I would certainly play them that way."

—John McGraw

"Tris Speaker was the king of the outfield. It was always 'Take it,' or 'I got it.' In all the years we never bumped each other."

—Outfielder / teammate Duffy Lewis

"Everybody has something to prove each year. Everybody has a responsibility in this game. Even the batboy."

—David Ortiz